Overcoming High-Tech Anxiety

Overcoming High-Tech Anxiety

Thriving in a Wired World

Beverly Goldberg

Jossey-Bass Publishers • San Francisco

Jossey-Bass books and products are available through most bookstores. To contact Jossey-Bass directly, call (888) 378-2537, fax to (800) 605-2665, or visit our website at www.josseybass.com. Substantial discounts on bulk quantities of Jossey-Bass books are available to corporations, professional associations, and other organizations. For details and discount information, contact the special sales department at Jossey-Bass.

 Manufactured in the United States of America on Lyons Falls Turin Book. This paper is acid-free and 100 percent totally chlorine-free.

Library of Congress Cataloging-in-Publication Data
Goldberg, Beverly.
    Overcoming high-tech anxiety : thriving in a wired world / Beverly Goldberg.—1st ed.
        p. cm.
Includes bibliographical references and index.
ISBN 0-7879-1022-8
    1. Employees—Effect of technological innovations on.   2. Employees—Effect of automation on.   3. Office practice—Automation. I. Title.
    HD6331 .G58 1999
    331.25—dc21   99-6309
                                                                        CIP

FIRST EDITION
HB Printing   10 9 8 7 6 5 4 3 2 1

The Jossey-Bass

Business & Management Series

Contents

Preface   xiii

1. Welcome to the New World   1

2. A Framework for Overcoming High-Tech Anxiety   11

3. Accepting the Constancy of Change   27

4. Understanding Today's Workplace   47

5. Gathering Knowledge from the Garden of Past Events   71

6. Networking: Making Critical Connections   95

7. Learning to Trust in Electronic Relationships   111

8. The Art of Reinvention   131

9. Looking Beyond Tomorrow   153

Notes   167

Acknowledgments   177

About the Author   179

Index   181

To my father
Solomon Goldberg (1913–1985)

Thank you for showing me the joy that can be found
in a world of books

Preface

> The simple fact is that we have come into a new
> world, and the charts of the world we used to live
> in no longer serve our needs. A new human society
> is being born. There are no new laws; but the law
> of Nature is the law of change, and new times
> necessitating a new attitude.
>
> —*Edward A. Filene*[1]

Edward Filene's "new world . . . necessitating a new attitude" was the machine age, the age of mass production that began in the 1920s. His words could apply just as easily to the beginning of any new era—the one we find ourselves in now, the information age, or the age of the industrial revolution, the bronze age, and so forth. As each period began, those who lived and worked in it had to deal with dramatic changes in the world around them that brought first uncertainty and then, as the world kept changing, anxiety. After a while, however, things settled down for a fairly long time. Moreover, those who lived through those earlier periods were usually unaware of what was happening until the changes affected their lives.

Today, almost no one can escape the constant, pervasive, and insistent barrage of news about how changes in information and communications technology are affecting every aspect of our lives and, especially, every aspect of the world of business. The reason the news is inescapable is that today we are all connected, whether it be by telephone, radio, television, or the latest in information and communications technology. Therefore, even if you are working in a field that you believe unlikely to be affected by rapid, unmanageable change, you know how quickly that belief can be proved wrong.

As a result, no matter how successful you are at the moment, you may well feel some degree of uncertainty about your future. Even if your current job seems secure, you cannot forget the downsizings of the late 1980s. Even if you have reached a high point in your career, you know you need a better grasp of how new technological developments will affect your company's business strategies for the future. Or perhaps you worry that if your company downsizes yet again you will need more technological skills than you currently have if you are to be one of the few offered the opportunity to stay on—and certainly you will need to acquire new skills to get that next job if you are let go. Or perhaps you just want to get ahead and recognize that without more technological skills that simply will not happen.

In other words, if you are a part of today's workforce and computers have not been a part of your life since childhood, you are probably worried about the impact future changes in technology will have on your life. At the same time, you find yourself hesitating to jump in and learn more. One part of you wants to believe the earthquake that shook the business world in the late 1980s and early 1990s is history. You want to relax and ignore the constant aftershocks technological advances are creating; it is just too much.

If you recognize yourself in any of this, this book is for you. It is designed to help you overcome your anxiety about technology and achieve success. It will provide you with the background to understand what has happened and what is likely to happen in the future, and then it will explain what you need to do to acquire the mind-set and tools that will guarantee your current and future employability.

Getting There from Here

Given the constant, breathless coverage of everything that computers can do, it may bother you that your skills are technologically limited. The world of work is now a world marked by constant changes.

Once you accept that fact, you have begun the journey. It need not be frightening. In fact, in many ways it will be rewarding, even exhilarating, because it offers a new frontier to explore.

Historically, people have always flourished when offered the opportunity for exploration and settlement of new frontiers. The electronic frontier offers such a world of opportunities and possibilities. A good way to think about it is to compare it to the opening of the American West. Here is your opportunity to go out and explore, and perhaps even settle in, a new land, one where the rules are not yet firmly in place, where what comes next is uncertain— and exciting. Cyberspace offers possibilities that at moments seem just as grand. Keep in mind that the opening of new frontiers is done in a series of incremental steps and that there is always difficult terrain to cross before you reach your goal.

You Can Take One Step at a Time

Nicholas Negroponte, one of the gurus of the wired world and the author of *Being Digital,* a book that offers a marvelous view of the information age, says early in the book that one of the questions he knew he'd be asked was, "Why an old-fashioned book . . . atoms instead of bits?" Here's the reason Negroponte offers for presenting his ideas in book form—the old-fashioned way: "There are just not enough digital media in the hands of executives, politicians, parents, and all those who most need to understand this radically new culture." Furthermore, he admits, "Even where computers are omnipresent, the current interface is primitive—clumsy at best, and hardly something with which you might wish to curl up in bed."[2] In other words, developing all the pieces and fitting them together do not happen overnight.

The road to electronic connectivity, however, is the subject of intense media hype: we are becoming a cashless society; trees are safe because we are on the verge of a paperless world; stores will be replaced by on-line shopping for everything we need; electronic connectivity will so widen the gap between the haves and have-nots that revolutions will result; everyone over thirty is bound to end up jobless (or worse, flipping hamburgers at minimum wage to survive); and people will soon live in isolation from one another, working from home, being entertained at home, rarely meeting face to face. In fact, the hyperbole you read and hear would make you believe the world is now totally different and that if you aren't yet a part of it, you are a failure. That simply isn't true.

What is true is that the hyperbole of those writing about this issue makes technological change seem overwhelming. If the stories in the media are accurate, technology has, for the past ten years at least, been making life on earth vastly different. However, my involvement in various ways with these issues over the past dozen years—both as a member of a think tank that explores such subjects and as a consultant helping organizations deal with the changes wrought by advances in communications and information technology—has made it clear to me that while enormous changes are taking place and will continue to take place in the ways that we connect, these changes will affect different aspects of our lives in different ways. The world as seen through the eyes of the devoted technophiles is not yet here.

On a personal level, there is time for each of us to decide how much a part of the electronically connected world we want to be. When it comes to the workplace, we have fewer choices. We must adapt—but adaptation and even mastery of this high-tech world that is constantly developing is not all that frightening if approached in the right way.

The reality of what is happening simply isn't as dramatic as predictions would have us believe. In fact, just as I began writing this book, I came across a review of a collection of books in the *Times Literary Supplement* headlined "No End in Sight." The conclusion of the article, which bemoaned the overabundance of books that predict great changes as new millenniums begin, said that "it is futile to expect such books to cease from appearing. What publisher ever laid out an advance for a book to be titled *The End Is Not As Nigh As All That?*"[3] I am lucky enough to have found such a publisher.

Indeed, the point of this book is that the new connectivity that is so ballyhooed as a sea change, a revolution, a new way of relating to one another and the world, is not quite here yet. We are in the midst of an ongoing evolution, one that is more difficult than most because the process is being enabled by technology; that is, technology is being used to create advances in technology. Moreover, the changes are taking place in two areas that have become interdependent—the way we collect and communicate information and the way business produces its products. Past changes in the collection and dissemination of information, such as printing and the telephone, and changes that affected production, such as electricity, have had enormous effects but did not converge in the same way.

The other added complication, of course, is that these changes are taking place not at midcentury, when they probably would receive less flamboyant commentary, but in the last decade of a century, the very years that are marked by a wealth of predictions about what the next century will bring. And because this century marks the end of a millennium, such prognostications have grown ever more abundant and extravagant.

We are a bit like children who expect their birthdays to be magical days, days in which they awaken perceptibly older—and different. But when they wake on that special day, they look in the mirror and are greeted by the same face they saw the night before. The same will probably be true in the first years of this eagerly awaited new millennium. The world will look no different from the world in which we went to sleep.

In reality, the world we wake to on any given day is another stage in an ongoing transition to a very different world than we could ever predict, not because of a single change that is taking place but because of the effects of the constant cascade of new developments that have been and are being initiated. What may happen during this new century is really anyone's guess, but it seems safe to say that the changes that will require the most adjustment and learning will be those brought by the convergence of the new information and communications technologies that connect us to one another in so many intimidating and exciting ways.

The difference between our experience and what happened to those who lived through earlier periods of change is mainly that they had less of a chance to see what was coming. When their lives changed, they dealt with it—but they did not spend as much time in a state of uncertainty about what might happen, one of the things most people find hardest to deal with.

The Road Ahead

The heart of this book is a framework for overcoming the anxiety brought by advances in technology by taking action. The action comes in the form of the six steps of the framework, six steps that will help you deal with the effects of technology on how you work. The philosophy underlying the steps of the framework contains answers to the following questions:

- What is the nature of the new technologies?
- What changes will they continue to bring?
- How will these technologies affect our concepts of, belief in, and actions regarding trust, honesty, and ethics?
- How will the changes brought by these technologies affect our relationships with others?
- What impact will these changes have on business and how will that affect us on a personal level?
- What do we need to do to adapt to these changes?
- What will happen to those who are left behind, disenfranchised from the future by lack of access to technology or appropriate education?

Although the developments that already have taken place have brought about changes in people's lives and in business, there is still time for you to master these new technologies. If you can overcome the tendency toward technophobia that afflicts so many, you will have the time not only to master the technology you need to succeed today but also to prepare for the technology that will change things yet again tomorrow.

Plan of the Book

The book begins with an explanation of why so many people are uncomfortable with, if not actually afraid of, the new information and communication technologies that seem to be omnipresent and have so changed the world of work. The second chapter then presents a framework consisting of six steps that will enable you both to understand the new world created by these technologies and to master additional technologically driven changes as they come along.

Chapters Three, Four, and Five, which are devoted to enhancing your understanding of what the new world of work looks like and means to you, take you through the first three steps of the framework. Chapter Three explores the need to accept change as a new constant in your life, Chapter Four explores the new world of work to help you decide where you fit in that world, and Chapter Five teaches you to keep alert to developments that might bring additional changes so you can avoid being blindsided by the future.

Chapters Six, Seven, and Eight, the last three steps of the framework, are designed to help you master the new technologies and acquire new skills when—and even before—you need them. Chapter Six explains how to network and use networks to your advantage, Chapter Seven explores the road to building trust that is key to the new connectivity that is a cornerstone of business success today, and Chapter Eight presents steps for acquiring technological skills.

Note that Chapters Three through Eight contain tips for actions related to the specific step addressed in the chapter.

The final chapter draws from its predecessors the answers to the questions presented earlier. I would suggest reading that chapter now—before delving into the book. It may prove difficult, but once you go through all the intervening chapters and read Chapter Nine again, you will realize that you already have begun to master this new world.

Chapter One

Welcome to the New World

> Would you realize what Revolution is, call it
> Progress; and would you realize what Progress is,
> call it Tomorrow.
>
> —*Victor Hugo*

In September 1998, 59 percent of respondents in a poll by two leading universities said that they were very concerned about job security for "those currently at work" and 28 percent said that they were "somewhat concerned."[1] This degree of anxiety makes clear how little the scars of the downsizings and displacements of the late 1980s and early 1990s have faded.

During that period, technology and competition from abroad eliminated hundreds of thousands of jobs in the steel, textile, and banking industries. Displaced middle managers in industry after industry were unable to find new jobs as organizations changed their structures in response to technological improvements that enabled better supervision and communication. Workers watched company after company downsize only to turn around and hire new workers with different skills—usually technology skills. As a result, worker resentment of corporate America grew, as did fears of technology.

The world of work was changing so rapidly that many workers began to fear that they never would master the new tools that seemed to change as fast as they learned how to use them. At the same time, the spread of technology was creating new businesses and something called the connected world, one that seemed the particular province of the young. Those not a part of this computer revolution felt somewhat betrayed—and very uncomfortable. Even if they were able to master enough technology to hold on to a job or secure a new one, change seemed to have become a way of life.

The changes that took place as a result of advances in information and communications technology affected not only their professional lives but their personal and civic lives as well. However, in those areas understanding and learning were and continue to be far less problematic than they are in the world of work, the world we must succeed in if we are to survive.

When it comes to our private lives, we can choose not to partake of these new advances at little cost. No one needs computers to communicate; there are telephones and the postal service. We don't need computers to purchase products; there are stores and catalogs. We don't need them for entertainment; books, television, movies, and games and activities of all sorts are abundant.

The world of work is the only area in which the effects of these changes are dramatic and inescapable. A revolution has taken place in the world of business. Large organizations have been forever changed, new businesses based on technology have become an important part of our economy, and when it comes to start-ups, not only are a good proportion of them technology based, but those that aren't find that using technology provides countless advantages, from simplified record keeping to accelerated collection of needed information.

All these changes, though devastating to those caught up in them, provided a spur to the economy and created an overall boom in jobs. Indeed, in the spring of 1998, only a short decade since these changes began to sweep corporate America, the unemployment rate reached a remarkably low 4.3 percent. Did that mean that all those affected in the beginning were once again whole? Had all those workers displaced by the onset of these changes become technology savvy?

To answer the second question first, many of the changes that result from the adoption of new technologies do not demand that workers become technologists but rather that they learn to use fairly simple forms of technology. Take, for example, an insurance adjuster who comes to examine a car that has been in an accident in order to determine the amount of damage. This person fills out a form on-site by writing on the screen of a small handheld device with a penlike instrument and then pressing a button to send the information to the home office's computer electronically. How different is this process from filling in the information needed on a paper form with a pen and bringing it back to the office? The job seems the same, but the person doing it has become part of the information age—a user of an "advanced communications device."

The answer to the first question is that many of those directly affected have permanently lost ground and may never be made whole. Some have had to face the fact that the jobs they had no longer exist; many have had to accept jobs that pay far less, while others have severely depleted their savings and pensions. Those who have found jobs know that these positions are not permanent and that they will need to acquire new skills or again face unemployment. And as we move further into the information age, demands for skills once thought the province of managers, such as communications and negotiating, now reach way down into the workforce, increasing the amount of learning everyone must do to be employable.

In addition, Flemming Larsen of the International Monetary Funds says that "over the period 1985–1995, real earnings of low paid workers . . . decreased by 5 percent in the United States. Skill-based technological change has probably been the main factor underlying the greater wage dispersion." But he adds that the "wage premium for the college educated doubled and workers who use a computer on the job now earn significantly more than those who do not."[2]

Given all of this, if you wake up in the middle of the night worrying about the possibility that a new technology your company is spending millions of dollars to buy will cost you your job or that your industry will be changed so radically by the advent of electronic commerce that your career will be threatened, you are not alone. The anxiety caused by technological advances can, however, be overcome. You can find your way in this new, continually changing world of work by taking the steps for overcoming high-tech anxiety that are the subject of the chapters to follow.

Before going on, uncovering some of the myths and realities about the effects of technological advances is a useful way to lessen anxiety and understand why there is so much distrust and fear of what it will bring—even among those who have achieved success in today's world of work.

Four Myths—and Realities

Number 1

Myth: Technological tools have grown increasingly complex and are impossible for people who are not technologically savvy to understand.

Reality: Appearances can be deceiving. Computers today are constantly being made easier and easier for people to use without specialized training. Perception is the problem. Indeed, if you look at a computer screen to see what it offers, you are presented with an overwhelming array of bells and whistles, including, at a minimum, for a relatively inexpensive machine, elaborate word processing and accounting programs, fax and e-mail capability, sophisticated games, CD-ROM, and programs to access the Internet. It doesn't matter that all you plan to use your computer for is correspondence or recording expenses. You can pick and choose what to use: that is, you can use e-mail without learning how to create a pie chart with the graphics program, and so on.

The business systems we read about and hear about involve an even greater array of mysterious possibilities, words that make little sense to many, such as data repositories and file servers; Ethernets and intranets; advanced workflow systems; trafficking, human resources, and financial programs; applications to design newsletters and even to illustrate books—the list seems endless. All you may use at the office is an application that tracks sales figures for your department and an e-mail system to help you reach those with whom you are working. But because you are faced with a menu presenting you with an incredible array of features, you feel you'll never be able to conquer this monster known as information and communication technology.

Remember that you have already learned to use the program that allows you to call up sales figures (you stuck Post-its to every corner of your terminal to be sure you remembered what the help desk had told you each time you called that first week, but slowly the notes fell off, never to be replaced). You can learn one new system at a time in the same way if you set your mind to it. If you were teaching a time traveler from the past how to use the telephone on your desk, you would go over how to dial a number and talk into the phone. You would not try to explain how to make a conference call, program speed dialing, or use any other features at the same time. The screen full of icons does not require instant learning.

Number 2

Myth: The real difference between the advances in technology taking place today and those of the past is that today's advances make products obsolete, destroying companies and people overnight.

Reality: Who doesn't know someone who lost a job—not because of being in an industry that was in a slump or working for a plant that moved to a new location but because the job disappeared? Draftsmen have been replaced by machines that produce blueprints with far greater speed and precision; commissioned insurance agents in the field are rapidly being replaced by minimum-wage customer service representatives who read scripts off their computer screens; the work of bank tellers, once a career path, is rapidly becoming the province of ATMs. This kind of change is not unique to the information age; automobiles brought an end to the careers of those who made horse-drawn carriages and buggy whips, but the automobile industry became a major employer that helped huge numbers of people achieve extremely comfortable lives. Jobs do disappear, but new ones are created—and for all the displacement unemployment is lower now than it has been in decades.

Keep in mind that radios and movies did not, as predicted, disappear with the introduction of television. Many so-called new products are merely improved versions of products already in existence, and they are being made by the same people.

Number 3

Myth: There are changes under way right now that are going to make the world unrecognizable tomorrow.

Reality: The reality here can best be explained in two parts. One, the media indulge in hyperbole when reporting on technological change, and two, change does not happen overnight, even if the technology that can bring it is already invented.

A good example of media hyperbole is the coming of the cashless society. In fact, the disappearance of money was reported as "taking place within the next five years" in 1980, 1981, 1982 . . . you get the picture. For years, futurists have been predicting a world in which we all sit in front of computers at home to do everything from work to shop to play, isolated from everyone else. To date, however, most attempts to move work from the workplace to home have met resistance. Some people do work at home at times— a small number do it close to full-time—but the disappearance of the traditional office building seems a long way off. Shopping centers and malls are not disappearing, and probably won't in our lifetimes, though they might be very different places in the future. People come to them to see and be seen, to touch and try on products. Is it any surprise then that the greatest successes when it comes to electronic commerce are books, stocks, and air travel?

Another area marked by extreme hyperbole is the Internet. For example, every time you turn on your television to watch the news, you're told to go to that channel's Web page for more information. After a while, you may believe you are the only viewer who doesn't do that. More and more people have home computers and are using the Internet; the increase in use is usually described as "exponential," but it is exponential only given its low starting point and the short time it has been widely available. Indeed, given statements such as "Use of the Internet doubles every year," it seems surprising to discover that surveys of Internet activity generally report usage ranging from 20 percent to 30 percent of the population.

Second, even if the constant announcements of the enormous developments were not exaggerated, the realities of implementation and economics would mitigate the problem. Keep in mind the words of Negroponte quoted in the Preface: "Even where computers are omnipresent, the current interface is primitive—clumsy at best, and hardly something with which you might wish to curl up in bed."[3] The development of a new technology does not necessarily result in its availability for instant use.

Nicolas Wade noted in the New York Times that "new technology is usually arduous to bring into being, since the steps leading from basic science to practical technology to acceptable product can each require heroic effort." Indeed, the reach of communications technology often means that the public becomes aware of the implications of those technologies long before they are out of the development phase. The result is a constant flood of information about changes that are "about to happen," many of which will not happen for decades, if at all. Wade says that "somehow the technology that's due tomorrow always seems far more profound and revolutionary than the high-tech products that arrived today."[4]

Number 4

Myth: We will all end up isolated from one another, sitting at home working, socializing, and communicating without ever coming face to face.

Reality: Although people do spend a great deal of time facing their computers instead of their friends and coworkers, especially when they first get computers, that tends to change with time, and much of the time spent replaces television viewing. Keep in mind that people are building relationships through this new technology. Groups form on-line to share interests and often the members of the group get together, setting up regional or even national events where they meet face to face.

When it comes to work, companies have already learned that face-to-face meetings are a necessary part of team building and other relationships that are conducted mostly on-line. Work at home has never reached the proportions it was expected to—and companies who allow it are constantly discovering the need to have regular meetings in headquarters with those who do work from home.

Thus although the changes we are dealing with today are likely to affect the way we build and conduct relationships—how we interact with other people—*interaction* is the operative word. "We are all connected," one telephone company assures us in its advertisements. Making sure that the connections enhance us rather than diminish us is something we will have to work on—but there are no signs that anyone wants connectivity without a human face.

Conclusion

The question of most concern for those of us engaged in the world of work is, What effects will these new technologies have on our own lives? That is, how will these new technologies affect business?

Once change was introduced into organizations in a very careful manner—sponsors would work at unfreezing a culture, helping people adjust to what was new, and then refreezing the culture for a period of time.[5] Today, the culture needed for continued business success is one of total flexibility—and so the message in business is constant change is the norm.

The only way to overcome the fears that this fundamental change has brought is to spend time learning everything you can about the new world of work and what it demands and what it offers—and then to acquire the understanding and knowledge and skills for success in that world. You must decide to spend your time learning instead of stalling, finding solutions instead of worrying.

We are living through a revolution, but if you follow Victor Hugo's words, you will call it progress—and progress is what will bring a better tomorrow. You can ensure your own success in the world of tomorrow by moving through the steps of the framework for overcoming high-tech anxiety.

Chapter Two

A Framework for Overcoming High-Tech Anxiety

Nothing in the world lasts
Save eternal change.
> —Honorat de Bueil, *seigneur de Racan*

Overcoming the anxiety brought by the avalanche of new information and communications technology requires understanding the effects of those technologies on the world, particularly on the world of work. Such an understanding will make clear the good that change can bring as well as the problems that often emerge in its immediate wake. It will help you find your own place in the new environment that results from any specific change, and yet keep you looking ahead to spot the next change coming.

On the national level, for example, we will have to be responding constantly to the economic, political, legal, and social ramifications of new ways of doing business, such as the various telecommunications acts and policies for addressing worker retraining and providing access for those too poor to acquire these technologies. On the corporate level, businesses must change their structures to be able to spot the next trend that may affect them, and they must be prepared to take advantage of the trends they spot before their competitors do. Employees, depending on temperament and where they are in their careers and life cycles, must either be prepared to learn and then learn again, reeducating and reskilling themselves constantly to be able to continue to provide value as each change comes along—or to find alternative paths.

Change Is Not Pain Free

While doing a benchmarking job at a hospital, I interviewed some-one in charge of admissions.[1] I'd been told he'd been with the hos-pital for three years and was one of the few people outside the technology group who felt comfortable with the hospital's new technological links to major insurers.

As the interview ended, I asked him how long he'd been doing hospital work, and he said, "Three years." I knew he'd been with that hospital three years, but had assumed he'd been in the field longer.

Curious, I asked if he'd join me for lunch to answer a few more questions. He hesitated, then agreed.

Once we were seated, I asked him to tell me what he liked about his work. He was far from forthcoming, and I told him that there was no need to answer and that I was sorry for taking his time, adding that it was curiosity that had prompted my questions.

He apologized and said that it was not me but that he just didn't feel like someone who should be talking about hospital work. I asked him why not, and he started talking.

A soft-spoken man in his early fifties, he said, "It's just that I don't know who I am anymore. My wife and I were at a party for her sister's anniversary this weekend—and her sister brought a cou-ple over and started introducing us, but she was called away. They sat down next to us, and the guy said, 'What do you do?'"

Shaking his head, he continued, "I don't know why, but I said, 'I'm a printer.'"

I asked how long he'd been a printer.

He paused, then said, "I think all my life. My father was a printer, but he wanted me to go to college. I tried it for a year because he wanted it for me so much. It just wasn't interesting to me. I'd been going to the shop with my Dad on weekends since I was a little kid. I just loved the smell of the ink, the look of the huge pages rolling off the press. So I dropped out of school and got a job in a print shop."

After a minute or so, he went on, "It was great. I loved my work. I made good money. I really liked it. . . . Then computers came along. Do you know what it's like in printing in New York today? There are no jobs. Shops are closing up all over the place. See, the small jobs are gone . . . flyers, brochures, reports are done on computers and photocopied. And New York isn't competitive. It costs too much, especially rent and salaries. . . . And now FedEx can send things overnight, so . . . work can go out of town. About five years ago, the last shop I worked in closed. I was the foreman. After a year of looking, I knew it was over."

I asked why he didn't move, and he explained that he had family responsibilities that kept him in the New York area. I then asked how he'd gotten into hospital work—and how he'd gotten as far as he had so quickly.

He said it was strange, but it was "because of the same thing that killed printing—computers." It turned out that while unemployed he spent a lot of time on his hobby, collecting old postcards. He was part of a couple of chat groups that communicated with one another through Prodigy, one of the earliest services for linking people by computer. Since he had the time, he took on the responsibility for arranging the group's annual national meeting.

The project turned out to be more complicated than he'd expected because his computer didn't have enough memory to handle the kind of communications program that would make arranging the meeting easy. When someone in the group heard about the problem, he mentioned it to someone else in the group who he knew was replacing her computer. When that person discovered her old computer was better than the printer's, she offered it to him. He gladly accepted the offer and soon found himself online exploring. He joined yet another group of collectors and began spending a lot of time writing electronic letters back and forth to someone he really liked.

"We discovered we live fairly close to one another and decided to meet. He works for a hospital in New Jersey."

During their second meeting, he told his new friend about his job problems. A few days later, his friend asked him if he could handle some overflow correspondence the hospital had. "He said it wouldn't pay much, but I grabbed it . . . anything would help. Money is money, and he said my letters to him were a lot better written than those he got from most of the people at the hospital who did that kind of work."

After a few months, he was asked to come to the hospital a couple of days a week. The result, in three years, was a career in hospital admissions. He had discovered that, he said, "a lot of things I did when I was foreman, like scheduling, reviewing contracts, estimating, were a lot like what it took to do this job. It doesn't pay as much, but I guess it's OK."

He got up to leave, adding, "The problem is, I'm really a printer—and printing is a dying industry, especially in New York City."

I said, "But first you said you didn't know who you were anymore."

"I guess I don't want to think of myself as part of the hospital—what if that disappears?"

Given the world of work today, he was right to anticipate more change. Reinventing oneself two, three, or even four times in the course of one's work life will be normal in the future. Successfully making those changes will require accepting the fact that change is now the norm.

The printer, a member of a family that had been in printing in New York for two generations before him, began his work life as so many others did, assuming he would retire as a printer. His story is far from unique.

At another hospital involved in the benchmarking project, I met a nurse who had been assigned to the Information Technology division to help develop a computerized scheduling system for the nursing department. Now, five years later, she was still working with the Information Technology department. In the course of our interview, she described herself as a nurse, grimaced, and said, "Well, I am a nurse. I just don't do nursing anymore. I haven't taken care of a patient in years. But at least I still work in a hospital."

These people are not unlike the farmers who were displaced by the coming of the industrial revolution. They had to adapt to survive. These people have not faced the life-or-death problems that those farmers and their children did. For the newly displaced, a strong economy, education, and the opportunity to acquire new skills helped them adapt and find work they could do successfully. The printer had unemployment checks for a time, some union support, and a retirement fund to tap into to tide him over; the nurse had never been out of work—she just wasn't doing what she expected and wanted to be doing. Both had to redefine themselves. Many of the farmers' families came close to starving, lost their homes, and soon broke up, some of the children moving to the growing mill towns dotted across the countryside, others emigrating.

Tales of downsized, displaced, and angry workers are easy to find. The stories of what happens to these people after the first year or two are not as common—perhaps because they are not as interesting. They are the stories of how people recovered, how they overcame what happened to them. Those are stories that provide the information we need to figure out how to prepare for the new, flexible world of work that makes the ability to learn and keep on learning the key to success.

The changes that take place in the world of work have costs. We can no longer assume that we are on a steady path to success because of our current skills. The printer is not earning as much as he did before. Even if he reaches that income level again, he has lost ground that he cannot regain, especially since he severely depleted his retirement savings. The nurse who added technological skills is doing better financially because her old skill set combined with her new one makes her particularly valuable to technologists who have to understand how hospitals work to design systems for them.

The printer's story, and the nurse's story, and hundreds of others taken together provided much of the information needed to develop a way for people—as well as businesses—to cope with the changes being brought by the advent of new technologies.

Embracing Change

No matter how often the point that change is inevitable and must be embraced is made, and no matter how much you steel yourself to accept change, the first reaction to change is fear. In the late sixteenth century, the political philosopher Machiavelli said: "It must be remembered that nothing is more difficult to plan, more doubtful of success, nor more dangerous to manage, than the creation of a new system. For the initiator has the enmity of all who would profit by the preservation of the institutions and merely lukewarm support from those who would gain by the new one."[2]

And yet, without the acceptance of change, success and forward progress is impossible.

Retailer and philanthropist Edward A. Filene said in 1935 that "there is no eternal principle more definitely established than the principle of constant change." What was true some two-thirds of a century ago is still true; what has changed is the speed with which change occurs. The exponential increase in the amount of change that is taking place lends force to Filene's belief that there are no patterns, no "normal years which could be effectively used as patterns for other years. . . . If times are good in one year and bad in another, it is not likely to be because we acted differently in one year than we did in the other. It is more likely to be because we did not see the necessity for acting differently and keeping up with the changing times. If we would only study change, instead of studying some transient aspect of it, change would not dismay us as it does. But not many of us have learned the art."[3]

What does the study of change itself, combined with the way people handle it, teach us? First and foremost, we see that while change causes unhappiness and disruptions—many large and unpleasant—eventually most people come to terms with it. Moreover, the people who have the easiest time doing so have developed habits that can be best described as stretching exercises aimed at maintaining mental flexibility and strength: habits that constitute a framework for overcoming high-tech anxiety (see Figure 2.1, p. 18).

The six steps in the framework will be addressed in great detail in the chapters that follow. They are far more complex than the catchwords used to describe them in the figure. In brief, the steps are as follows:

- *Reaching acceptance:* Acknowledging the constancy of change
- *Achieving understanding:* Learning what the new world of work is and finding a place in it
- *Gathering knowledge:* Discovering what the future may hold through an examination of the past
- *Networking:* Exploring how to build the critical connections with people and organizations that are necessary for success in the new world of work
- *Building trust:* The key to establishing the kinds of relationships that ensure success in the new world of work
- *Reinvention:* Acquiring the new skills and developing strategies for future success

The first step in using the framework is to understand what each element entails and how each is linked to the others. The second is to remember that many of the steps can be done simultaneously; the point here is not to stop continuing to, say, accumulate knowledge while you are working on reinventing your skill sets. The goal is to keep all the steps in mind and constantly restart the process, which is why it is presented in the form of a wheel. Because it is an ongoing, iterative process, it drives constant reevaluations that help you stay aware of and responsive to change.

To return to the printer for a moment, think about the things that made his new role in life possible. He had comfort with and a

Figure 2.1   Framework for Overcoming High-Tech Anxiety

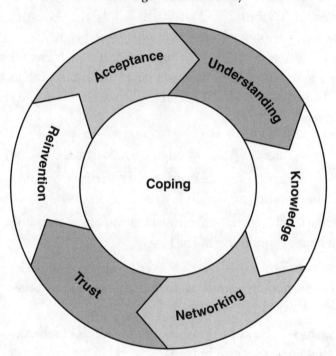

basic *understanding* of how to use technology, which he gained as part of his pursuit of a hobby. He had learned to know how to *trust* on-line so he could *network* with people, specifically in this case the networking with the woman who gave him the computer that allowed him to expand his network so that he met the man who actually got him into hospital work. He had a skill base to use to *reinvent* himself—the ability to communicate well and scheduling and contract skills that proved transferable. He had *accepted* the need to change—and he knows change is likely to affect him again. If he begins to acquire *knowledge,* about the changes taking place in health care in his area, he can begin to try to figure out the next move to make, and begin to move through the steps again. The trip should be easier this time.

The Six Steps

Acceptance.   Once you reach the point of competence in a new skill, once you have mastered the world as it is today, you have about a nanosecond to enjoy your accomplishment. You have reached a new level, but more changes will come to change things again. Imagine a tabletop; now picture a bucket of sand with a small hole in the bottom hanging high over it. As the grains of sand fall, a mound builds up. At some point, however, an avalanche occurs and the surface once again becomes level. As the sand continues to fall, the process is repeated time and time again. Today, there is always another grain of sand about to drop, creating yet another mountain for you to climb. However, as the possessor of new skills, you have bought yourself time to begin again, while staying on a fairly high level.

Recognizing and accepting the fact that change is a constant is a key to success. Pacing yourself so you are doing well and enjoying life and your success while preparing for the next cycle is the way to remain as stress free as possible. Remember that although you will have to continue to change, you can take charge and make the decisions about when to take the next step—and sometimes take multiple steps, continuing to build knowledge while learning new skills.

Understanding.   The world of work has been changed dramatically by information and communication technologies, which flatten formerly hierarchical organizational structures, bring an emphasis on teamwork, and demand that everyone have skills such as communications and negotiations that were once the province of middle managers. Organizations have become far more flexible, maintaining a smaller core workforce at times, and then expanding rapidly when opportunities for growth present themselves. This not only means that permanent full-time employment is no longer a norm, but it means that those who do have such jobs need to be able to train temporary, contract, and new workers so that they apply their skills to the organization's specific requirements and understand the organization's culture.

Along with a shrinking core workforce in the largest organizations has come a growth of smaller businesses; in fact, small businesses created an astonishing number of jobs in the early 1990s. The U.S. Small Business Administration reports that firms with less than one hundred employees hired almost 10 million workers in that period, firms that employed from one hundred to five hundred workers accounted for 8.5 million new jobs, and the largest firms (those employing more than five hundred workers) reduced their employment rolls by a little over 3 million.[4] Many of these small organizations, which are set up to meet the outsourcing needs of larger organizations, offer far different kinds of employment—contract, at-home, part-time, temporary—and few benefits.

In a world where work has so many new definitions and structures, employees must define the kind of employment they are seeking and adjust that definition as they enter different phases of their life cycle. Along with the expansion of choice that comes with organizational flexibility comes increased responsibility. Workers in large organizations must hone their specific skills even if they have moved into more managerial roles, and if they have not moved to that level, they must acquire general managerial skills—such as writing, presenting, negotiating—while sharpening the specific skills they were hired for, say, design or accounting. Workers in small organizations cannot count on being given training in the new technology they must use to communicate with the larger companies that are their employers' important clients—they must acquire it themselves. Workers who choose to work at home have to learn to self-start and pace themselves. Understanding the differences this new world of work has made in the nature of jobs is essential for success.

Knowledge.   There are two aspects of knowledge to keep in mind here—context and content. Chinese philosopher Lao-tzu, writing in the sixth century B.C., pointed out that "to know one's ignorance is the best part of knowledge." In other words, if you know the limitations of your knowledge, you can work to augment and build on that knowledge instead of working to build basic understanding.

Today, when so much information is available, most of us have learned to filter out what doesn't interest us or is unlikely to affect us, file what adds to our knowledge, or find out more about what is new and confusing. The problem isn't a lack of information to sort through; indeed, "A weekday edition of *The New York Times* contains more information than the average person was likely to come across in a lifetime in seventeenth-century England," according to Richard Saul Wurman in *Information Anxiety*.[5] The problem is to determine which pieces of information are important and figure out the most useful ways to acquire and analyze that information so that it moves to the next level—knowledge.

Analysis requires context; each piece of information you acquire about developments taking place in the world needs to be measured—compared to and analyzed in terms of the history of other developments to determine what effect it might have. The easiest way to do that is to look at similar categories of developments in the past. This helps you determine the probable magnitude of the changes that might result from current developments. The context you use for this analysis and comparison is the general knowledge about history, science, the economy, politics, and society that you have acquired over the years. The process of analysis involves asking yourself questions and speculating about possibilities.

In other words, look for stories about new developments in your industry or area of expertise in the media (keeping in mind how prone the media are to exaggeration), listen to people who have a good track record, and reflect on what they have done and how they've done it. Play with ideas—try to do your own brainstorming and brainstorm with others.

Although you may not need that information to do your job today, it is almost certain you will need it tomorrow. What effect will a given development have on the need for employees, the structure of the company, the various business processes it uses? It's worth keeping track of and assessing developments in technology by asking yourself such questions. It will keep you from being totally surprised in the future. Even though you might not have arrived at exactly the right answer, you will have the comfort of knowing you at least forecast a change. Moreover, even if you don't need this information for career purposes because you are retiring in a few years, you will need it as a citizen and a member of society.

Knowledge is a great strengthener; it helps reduce unwarranted anxiety and points the way to appropriate reactions.

Networking.   Building relationships, personal and professional, is the basis of networking, the process that begins when you ask someone you have grown to know and begun to trust to do something or when you are asked to do something by that person. It may be someone you know because you worked together raising funds for your children's school now asking you to serve on a committee, provide information about an opportunity, size up a situation, or make an introduction. After a time, one of you introduces the other to someone else you know, and your personal network expands. Building such networks allows you to accomplish more than you can on your own.

Now there are new technologies that can enhance your ability to network. These electronic networks—systems built to connect the members of organizations to one another—have become critical in many parts of the business world. You have to learn how these networks actually work, what is involved in using them, and what dangers and opportunities they present. You also have to learn to manage the relationships that underlie these new business networks to avoid problems that can undermine the new connectivity. A critical part of this learning is deciding who the stakeholders are when organizations are joined electronically. You have to learn how to team up with people you've never met and have to find ways to build mutual understanding—which is exactly what the next step is about.

Trust.   Because the ways in which relationships are established are undergoing dramatic changes, the issue of trust has taken on a new dimension. You may find yourself working in teams, having to deal with others because of partnerships and strategic alliances, and building relationships with clients on-line. In the absence of the opportunity to get to know people face to face or track down the sources of information posted, reputation becomes an increasingly important guide to decision making.

In the past, when you heard something that cast doubt on an individual or company, in addition to checking their reputation for honesty, integrity, and ethical behavior, you could spend some time with them, gauging their answers to questions and their reactions to statements through intonation and body language. Today, you will either have to hold them to higher standards of reputation or find new ways to determine trustworthiness.

In business, the difficulties created by the issue of trust are inescapable when organizations are placing greater reliance on communication technology as a routine way of conducting business. Today, many uses of technology that have been proven to increase profitability require the sharing of information electronically, which often means allowing others access to systems that contain confidential information, a risky situation that raises the issue of trust in a different way: How much do you trust another organization to have put in place the proper security to protect your organization?

There is also the issue of trust and ethics in terms of outsourcers and temporary workers, many of whom work for a number of competing companies because of their very narrow but urgently needed skills. Rules of ethical governance, clear explanations of expectations, and a mutual belief in one another's integrity will be critical to making these relationships work.

Reinvention.   Once you come to terms with the fact that the changes taking place will have an effect on you, once you understand the need to find ways to develop trust, once you have an idea of the things that new technologies can do, you are ready to take the next step—developing new proficiencies. Training in new skills is the critical step to continuous employment.

Information and communication technologies change so quickly today that even the experts feel it is impossible to keep up. The key to overcoming your anxiety is understanding that, for most of us, surviving in business does not require knowing anything about how applications are coded or how a new piece of hardware is assembled. What we need to know is what information it provides. We need to ask ourselves, How can we use that information in different ways to gain an advantage? How do we prepare our report on the finances in our department on a spreadsheet? How do we use it to present a report? How do we make the e-mail system work? In other words, we need to learn to use the computer as a calculator, a typewriter, a research tool, a fancy all-in-one phone and fax machine.

Since it is a rare office indeed that hasn't computerized some functions, begin to look around even if your department doesn't do much with computers now. Ask a colleague for a chance to learn what a new program does; read books about how technology changes the workplace; go to a library, community center, or computer store offering Internet access and play around or watch others explore the Internet and see what it offers.

Watching technology in action is a relief for most people. It makes what seemed mysterious less frightening. The realization of how easy today's systems are to use goes a long way toward easing fears about plunging in and exploring technology. The streams of commands once necessary to perform the simplest operation have been replaced by icons that even the uninitiated understand.

Furthermore, computers are likely to become even easier to use in the future, as computer companies, facing resistance from those who have not already entered this new world, face up to the need to entice new customers. Clare-Marie Karat, of IBM's Thomas J. Watson Research Center, offers this warning for the computer industry: "The profile of the people who use systems has changed, while the systems, and the culture in which they have developed, have not adjusted."[6]

The changes will not happen overnight, however, so if you decide you want to be a player in this new world of business you are going to have to devote serious attention to constantly finding opportunities to acquire training in the skills that are in demand.

A Problem for the Future

Before moving on to explore the six steps in the framework, it might be wise to think about a problem that may loom larger than the immediate problem of personally overcoming the anxiety created by high technology. You are not the only one who has to find a way to learn new skills. All the frameworks in the world will be useless if our economy falters in the next decades because of a lack of skilled workers.

The problem America is facing is one of demographics as well as education. When the baby boom generation of some 76 million retires in the first half of the twenty-first century, it will be replaced by the baby bust generation of some 56 million. In a world of fewer workers, having skilled workers and being able to train people in new skills becomes critical. Not only must we adapt to this new world, we owe it to ourselves to make sure that tomorrow's workers are ready for it.

In 1995, Secretary of Education Richard W. Riley warned that "whether or not schools invest in technology, children from affluent and middle-income families will enjoy access to the latest technologies in their homes—including powerful personal computers and peripheral devices such as CD-ROMs, scanners, printers, modems, and network connections. State and local leaders should insist that schools in the lowest-income neighborhoods be the first to be provided with the latest technologies."[7] This is not happening, however. In late 1996, if you overlaid a map showing the spread of technology to schools on one showing the average income of school districts, you would see that the poorest children were in the districts with the least technology. We simply cannot afford to allow any of the workers of the future to be undereducated. After all, even though you are worried about your current and next job, you need to look ahead to the time when you will no longer be working but will depend on a sound economy for a comfortable retirement.

Conclusion

The time has come to move on to the first step of the framework, acceptance—that is, acceptance of the fact that frequent change is part of the business world today. As companies become learning organizations, flexible organizations, connected organizations, the jobs they offer change to match the structures put in place to enable them to respond as quickly as possible to changes in market demand. That means you must always be ready, willing, and able to change if you want to remain employable. The burden has been put squarely on the worker in this new world of work. With time, and tighter labor markets as the baby boomers retire, companies may well have to accept more responsibility for workers. For the moment, however, the responsibility—fair or not—is yours.

Chapter Three

Accepting the Constancy of Change

Expectations of the future shape action in the
present.

—*Charles Heckscher*[1]

Do you expect the future to bring even greater technological
advances? If you do, you have taken the first step to acceptance. Do
you believe that those changes will come so rapidly that you are
likely to be affected by them? If you have learned new skills and
found new employment and your income is beginning to approach
the level it was before the last round of changes, you are probably
reluctant to face the fact that the next round that will affect you is
already under way. You simply want a chance to relax and enjoy
what you have achieved.

True acceptance—the first step of the framework for overcoming the anxiety constant technological advances cause so many of
us—involves admitting to yourself that whatever has happened, no
matter how tumultuous it has been, has been a single event in a
chain of events. You reach true acceptance only when you are
watching for the next set of changes even when in the midst of
dealing with the current set. Thus acceptance involves being so
certain that change will come that you decide to take action now
to prepare for it. It means setting out—and following—a program
of continuous learning, frequently reassessing your current industry
and job and skills, constantly expanding and refining your networks, and preparing both financially and psychologically for the
next upheaval. It means acknowledging change is now the norm.

No Rest for the Weary—And Who's Weary, Anyway?

Part of acceptance is giving up the idea that there will be any stage of your work life when you can sit back, ignore new developments, and wait for retirement, perhaps actually retire. If you do so, you are closing yourself off far too soon. After all, most people who reach retirement age today can expect more than a dozen years of active and healthy living. And even when you reach retirement, you may be affected by change. For example, inflation or a change in family circumstances may mean that you need to get back into the workforce at least part time to augment your retirement income (most Americans have not saved enough for a comfortable long retirement). If you do, knowing at least something about technology will be critical. For example, Florida-based Home Shopping Network hires many senior citizens to serve as part-time customer service representatives. They use computers to check inventory when taking orders, entering those orders, and then forwarding them to the company's warehouse, billing department, and so forth.

Even if you do not rejoin the paid workforce, you may—as many people do—look forward to retirement not only as a time to rest from the grind of a full-time job but as a time to give back to the community through volunteer work. Today, since hospitals, schools, and political and environmental organizations are already so computerized, you are likely to contribute more the more computer skills you have, especially when it comes to fundraising activities. (Volunteer work need not wait until retirement; you can help yourself as well as others by volunteering—when you do you expand your networks and often have an opportunity to build new skills.)

Simply put, the new connectivity is being adopted so quickly that it is unlikely you can—or will want to—avoid it. For example, DFI Incorporated, a Washington, D.C., research organization evaluating the new connectivity for the military, noted:

During the summer of 1997, the USS *John F. Kennedy* carrier battle group provided 8,000 sailors with free e-mail access during a deployment to the Mediterranean

- Over 1.7 million e-mail messages were sent and received over the six month deployment
- Internet access provided for personal use to sailors; up-to-date homepage maintained so family members can find out the latest of battle group activities.[2]

The implications of those 1.7 million messages are enormous. The people involved in receiving this abundance of e-mail and information on-line were not the parents of students attending major universities or the U.S. relatives of employees of overseas branches of large corporations: they were the families of people serving in the military—average Americans—connected Americans.

Millions of Americans of various ages already use e-mail and the Internet at home and at work. Although many believe it is a tool of the young because they were somehow born to it, or that the video games they played as they were growing up and the presence of computers in so many schools is what makes it easy, it is not true. Older people are also turning to it—45 percent of home users surfing the Net are over the age of forty[3]—as new developments make it easier and easier to use these once difficult devices.

Many turn to the new connectivity out of curiosity mixed with a great deal of anxiety, and a desire to see what is causing such excitement. Charles McGrath, a *New York Times* editor, says, "Like most people of my generation—people who grew up in the 1950s and 60s, with books and typewriters—I began exploring the Internet partly out of curiosity but mostly out of fear. If, as the techies and the zealots keep telling us, the Net is the world of the future, the place where we will work and play and think and socialize, I wanted to know what this brave new world was like. What I discovered, not really to my surprise, is that the Net is all too much like the world we already live in."[4]

For many who turn to them, computers primarily serve as just another form of communication; others use them for research, fun, browsing and buying, meeting like-minded people—and more and more are discovering new uses, no matter what their original intentions. The speed with which people are adopting this technology for private use is remarkable, far surpassing the speed with which new technologies were adopted in the past (see Table 3.1).

Of course, various external forces play a role in determining how fast something will be adopted: for example, when it came to television and radio, increased demand depended on the availability of content. The telephone did not become an overnight sensation because there was little point in owning one until enough people you wanted to reach also owned one. In fact, the telephone took twelve years from its first entry into homes at the turn of the century to reach the level the Internet did in only five years. If the trend toward increased speed of penetration of new technologies continues, the next wave of innovation could be adopted even more quickly—although it will never happen overnight.

A Sampling of the State of Tomorrow

The changes brought by technology have affected the world of work far more rapidly than any other area because that world is

Table 3.1 The Spread of Technology

Technology	Year Invented	Years to Reach 20 Percent Penetration	Penetration in 1997 (Percentage)
Electricity	1873	42	98.8
Telephone	1876	32	93.9
Radio	1906	26	97.8
Television	1926	25	98.3
Microwave	1953	29	84.1
Personal computer	1975	14	40.0
Internet access	1991	5	26.0

Source: Adapted from Forbes, July 7, 1997, pp. 170–172, based on calculations by W. Michael Cox of the Dallas Federal Reserve Bank.

focused on the bottom line—and technology increases efficiency. However, neither government nor other institutions are immune; indeed, the adoption of advanced technology by government and the turmoil in higher education reveal a lot about the future.

The results of the attempts of federal and local governments to adopt advanced technologies are very uneven. The Internal Revenue Service has had well-publicized problems getting its new information systems up and running, as has the Federal Aviation Agency. Many local government Web sites do little more than provide descriptive, promotional material and announcements of meetings. New York City, however, provides a fairly sophisticated, interactive Web site that makes it possible for taxpayers to "fill out a complaint about a broken light or electronically file any one of 11 different online forms."[5] Camden, New Jersey, has successfully implemented a program that provides needy families with their food stamp benefits and cash subsidies through an ATM-type system.[6] Many other communities are in the process of following suit.

At the same time, H. Ross Perot's much-discussed electronic town hall, which led to speculation about the possibility that voters would one day engage in frequent referendums about important national issues, is still clearly a long way off. Even if the technology were available, the disadvantages outweigh the excitement—which was more over the possibility of doing so than the wisdom of doing so. While the idea of using electronic responses to gauge the mood of the moment is a boon to pollsters and lobbyists, it does not mesh with the precepts of our democracy, which require thoughtful analysis of issues and fair representation.

When it comes to education, particularly higher education, the effects of technology are interesting for a number of reasons. First, the growing national concern over and resistance to the constant increases in the costs of education have made it necessary for colleges and universities to rethink the model in place. Second, technology has made possible alternative models that can supplant the current model or be integrated into it. Third, the effects of technology on business has created a need for a new type of education—and with changes, these institutions can fill that role.

Given all this, the world of higher education has to change not only to survive but to try to survive while retaining what many believe to be the most valuable vestiges of its past. Peter Drucker, a management expert with a long history of accurate forecasts of the future, recently predicted that "information technology will bring about the demise of the university as currently constituted. Insofar as the university's physical manifestation is a response to scarcity—the scarcity of great minds capable of imparting what they know—the Internet logically renders its continuation in that form redundant."[7]

Bear in mind that the demise he is forecasting is of the university's physical form. Even here, the change need not be so dramatic if these venerable institutions can find ways to meet the immediate needs of today's students while making the case for the values inherent in the current system. Many look at the recent advances in communications and information technology and ask, Why not have teleconferenced classes where the experts in each field teach huge groups of students across the country? Why shouldn't students attend virtual institutions charged with the responsibility for seeing to it that they complete a course of study that meets the criteria for a degree?

There is a model that provides just what the people asking those questions are looking for—the University of Phoenix, which was founded in the mid-1970s and offered shares on the NASDAQ exchange in 1994. Now one of the largest universities in the nation in terms of enrollment, it has forty-seven sites in the West, Florida, Louisiana, and Michigan. These sites, which serve as the equivalent of campuses, are physically little more than some office space in buildings close to highway entrances and exits. The *New Yorker* reports that the university also lacks tenured professors and most of the other things we associate with universities, including a bureaucracy.

The president of the university, William Gibbs, says that "the people who are our students don't really want the education. They want what the education provides for them—better jobs, moving up in their careers, the ability to speak up in meetings." In other words it provides, often through distance learning—learning done on-line, at home, whenever convenient—tools aimed at ensuring employability.[8]

In some ways the University of Phoenix and its smaller clones are not as startling a development as one would immediately think: only a sixth of the fourteen million people currently engaged in pursuing higher education in the United States are full-time students living on campus. According to Diana G. Oblinger and Sean C. Rush of IBM, who are involved in that company's educational programs, "The most likely future is one which accommodates more options for learners. Residential colleges and universities will still be in demand for many learners. However, technology expands the reach and range of those traditional settings. Hybrid organizations may be formed where students can synthesize on-campus with on-line experiences. Other students, particularly working adults, may opt for on-line experiences that provide them with the education and flexibility they need."[9]

In other words, the changes that are taking place in the universities because of technology will provide numerous benefits for those who find they have to add new skills to ensure their future. That approach, however, ignores a number of the purposes of the university as presently constituted. There is a role played by universities that we can ill afford to abandon—a setting that allows students to engage in extensive exchanges of ideas with others, to explore, to grow independent, to learn how to learn, and to make connections for the future. It also has a role in training the educators of tomorrow that requires the kind of setting just described.

The only way to preserve the traditional roles of the university is for those who work in higher education to accept the fact that they must change. They must stop focusing on the threats to tradition and instead find ways to provide more people with the kinds of education they need. Resisting any change is the worst path they can choose. Virtual universities can provide the bare minimum of specific skills for advancement, but the richness of information that people have become aware of opens on-line education to more than that. It is up to those in the university to find ways to provide a broad enough range of types of education to protect the core values for which the universities were created. Educators must learn to walk the line between the "two great traditions pushing up against one another. One argues that the pursuit of knowledge for its own sake creates fully rounded men and women with sharp enough minds to succeed at anything they attempt. The other tradition contends that the pursuit of practical knowledge, particularly the scientific, sharpens the mind as effectively as the study of Greek and Latin, and addresses the broad needs of the people."[10]

Some have begun, adding programs that involve distance learning to try to retain their enrollment numbers. This is a promising effort—as retraining becomes more and more a part of life, it should increase enrollments. Professors are already learning how to teach at a distance and are helping publishers develop textbooks suitable for on-line learning, particularly in the sciences. Of course, anxiety levels are rising as the message that nothing is permanent breaches the walls of these ivory towers. If, however, any place can adjust, it will be the very place where learning to learn is a mantra. A failure here will have adverse affects on all of us because these institutions are part of the key to the continuous learning everyone must undertake.

You should keep the changes affecting our educational institutions in mind as you begin to consider the next steps to take to ensure your future because the changes affecting these institutions are a model for the changes brought by technology. In addition, these institutions may play a critical role in providing you with the skills you need in the future.

Next Steps

Once you reach the point where you expect change, you are ready to embark on a course of constant action to prepare for the next set of changes, which you can be sure is on the way even if you can't predict its shape. Begin by making the steps of the framework a part of your routine and embark on a program of continuous skill acquisition whether you plan a new career or want to move ahead in the one you now have. Taking action reduces anxiety—it leaves you with less time to worry and gives you a feeling of control.

Remember that no matter how involved you are in your present job, even if you were hired because you already had added to your existing skill set, you cannot sit back and relax. More changes are already taking place. For example, merger and acquisition activity has risen to new heights and is likely to remain high through the early years of the millennium. As a result, according to a 1997 survey by Robert Half International of Menlo Park, California, 51 percent of executives rank "loss of jobs due to acquisition or merger" as their number one concern. This figure represents a one-year jump of 6 percent.[11]

The nature of the new world of work is such that once you understand it, you will realize why you must not take the steps of the framework in Figure 2.1 sequentially. You must make at least two activities, accumulating information and reaching out, a lifelong habit.

Accumulating Information

To make sure you are informed about new developments and their possible impact, understand the changes taking place in the world of work, and know what skills you should acquire, you must begin to make a habit of accumulating information about new developments. The demands of the new world of work do not leave a lot of time for this, but you owe it to yourself to make some time to read the Sunday edition of your paper, especially if it provides a section devoted to a review of the week's news. A magazine such as *Business Week*, *Fortune*, or *Forbes* is another good way to follow developments that will have an impact on business. Some of the national all-news television channels have segments on trends in business and technology; find out when they are broadcast in your area and watch them carefully. Subscribe to at least one magazine aimed at your profession and one aimed at your industry. (This last can be part of the next step.)

Reaching Out

Building networks and establishing trust fit together very neatly. In part, the more you can find out about organizations and people, the easier it is to begin a relationship with as few doubts and fears as possible. Join professional organizations, and keep in mind that membership usually includes a subscription to a magazine, which goes to the last point about collecting information. For example, if you are in human resources and specialize in training, the Association of Training and Development's *Training & Development* is part of your membership package; if you are in management, it is the American Management Association's *Management Review* that comes free with membership. Remember that it is not enough to join these groups—participate in order to build networks that will keep you informed.

You also should think about joining chat groups whose members are involved in the same area of business you are. And once you are on-line, look up placement agencies just to get ideas about the national as well as local job market. Note what skills are paying well. If you are not on-line, you can do some of this through your newspaper, but be aware that the picture you are getting is local.

Don't Drift—Think About Your Careers

For most people, getting a job with a decent salary, benefits, and a chance to move ahead provides a feeling of security that allows for relaxation. After a while, they might look around and think about switching to another company. Sometimes when a colleague moves on to something that sounds exciting, they begin to think about making a change. More often, in the past decade, the sight of consultants trooping in and out, low or no quarterly profits, and a fall in the price of the company's stock served as the wake-up call people needed to make them think about their careers. Of course, actually taking some action once the scent of danger is in the air is often stalled by the instinct to spend far more time at work to prove your value to the company, to make sure you are in the group that isn't asked to leave.

As with so many other things in life, we procrastinate about job development, dealing with things only when we have to. Christine Furler, president of CareerNet of Morristown, New Jersey, says that it is her experience that "most people take better care of their cars than they do their careers."[12] The time when that was possible has passed. You need to get in the habit of assessing your career at set intervals.

Mary Anne Rust, a clinical psychologist who directs the Success Training Institute in Woodland Hills, California, says that you must "look around and recognize that no matter how well things seem to be going for you, it could change and change for the worse—it's the one constant in the workforce today. . . . Employees from the shop room to the board room are moved out or pushed out."[13] The problem with avoiding the possibilities, with not looking around and preparing, is that when you have no choice, you grab whatever job you can find.

As you think about your job path, you are really thinking about a career. That is fine, as long as you keep in mind that today you are likely to have a number of careers. You might end up moving through three jobs during one of your careers; then you might make a move to a new career by developing new skills, and once again pursue a career path. Since the world of work, as we will see in the next chapter, is changing so rapidly, and we are on average living so much longer, two or three careers each lasting from a dozen to two dozen years is a distinct possibility. The reason for approaching work in career terms is that with each step ahead in a career, you acquire more skills, many of them transferable. The printer described in Chapter Two was able to use his skills in scheduling and communicating to build a new career in hospital administration. The nurse's knowledge of hospitals made her valuable in the world of computer programming.

There are a few simple steps that will help you focus on the concept of careers rather than sequential jobs:

• *Assess your job every six months.* Ask yourself whether your company seems stable and whether your department is performing efficiently. Then ask yourself whether you could stand doing what you are doing for the next seven years, whether you are growing and learning, and whether there are opportunities ahead. Finally, ask yourself to rate your work-happiness quotient on a scale of one to ten and write the number on a piece of paper and stick it in a file with your résumé. In six months, when you do it again, check that the number is at least the same; if it is lower, even if everything else seems okay, it is time to move on.

• *Keep your résumé current.* Pull it out every few months (at least twice a year) and add every new skill you have learned and describe every project you have completed. Make sure it includes general skills such as writing, scheduling, and teamwork as well as specific skills such as engineering, research, or capabilities with specific technologies. If the list looks skimpy, take some courses to add to it.

More important, review the objectives you have stated and the description of the kind of job you want. Do they really reflect what you want or are they simply the standard list? Do they reflect where you are in your work and life cycle? Do not fall into the trap of advancement as the only goal. You might want to do something at your current level but in another area—of the company or the country. Spend some time thinking about what you want to be doing.

• *Explore job listings.* Get in the habit of looking at the classified job advertisements in your newspaper every week. Looking over the whole section is important because it will give you a sense of the changes that are taking place. Examining what is happening in your area will help you determine whether the field you are in is in trouble. (On-line job listings are particularly valuable tools for broader geographical searches, another reason for adopting these new technologies.)

Every six months, go through all the listings in the Sunday paper and circle every job that looks interesting—no matter what field it is in. See if the jobs that intrigue you have something in common. For example, are they all jobs that require research skills or are they all in a specific industry? Also try to determine what additional skills you would need to be the right candidate for the jobs you selected—it may inspire you to action.

• *Build relationships with recruiters.* You should reach out to recruiters well before you have any intention of looking for a new job. Explain that although you are not yet ready to move, you would like to begin to talk and that in return you are willing to help them by suggesting candidates for positions that they are trying to fill. If you have built such connections, you will find that over time, the discussions of your current job will lead to suggestions—of openings you would be qualified for "if only you also had skills in x or y." These conversations may provide just the push you need to begin to add new skills. More important, these relationships will serve you well when it is time to look for a new position.

Is Going High-Tech the Answer?

When you begin to think about moving into a new career, the word *technology* is likely to be the first that occurs to you. After all, the newspapers are filled with stories about the more than a hundred thousand high-tech jobs going begging, about the corporate recruiters luring college students off the degree path, about the industry's efforts to get the government to allow more immigrants with these skills into the country. If you are going to have to learn how to use these new technologies to survive, maybe you should go all the way?

First, remember that learning to use an application is quite different from learning to build one. How long a course of study are you willing to embark upon? Look into the kind of training both high-tech companies and those who supply workers to those companies on a contingent basis are offering. If you have particular industry expertise, for example, you might find it easier to get into such a program aimed at bringing high-tech support to your industry.

There are a number of reasons moving into high tech could be a valuable step in building your career. *Business Week* reports that "there's a new career calculus that makes a shift into high tech the right move for many executives and professionals in their 30s, 40s, and 50s. The booming high tech sector is creating 40 percent of all new managerial and professional positions outside of health and education. . . . A stint in the high tech sector can give a major boost to your long-term career prospects, even if you don't stay in high tech. Tech companies are shaping up to be the prime training ground for the next generation of CEOs and senior executives for the rest of the economy."[14]

Basically, a move into high tech makes the most sense for those who are fascinated by technology and believe that is where the excitement and the future are. Others may make the move because the high-tech industry provides the opportunity to work in a place where creativity and innovation are encouraged, where things happen quickly, where there are few rules and regulations and little sense of hierarchy. Others are attracted primarily by the possibility of getting rich; they are willing to take the risk of a low salary now for the stock options that will bring rewards later.

Embarking on a Continuous Improvement Program

Even though, according to the second *Towers Perrin Workplace Index*, "94 percent of respondents agree it is their responsibility to remain employable by continuing to learn new job skills,"[15] far too many people manage to put off taking action. The people who do so even when they can see that the shape of the future makes such action inevitable are the ones most likely to have problems when the next set of changes takes hold.

Do not fall into the trap the financial officer of a major mid-western teaching hospital did. In the course of an interview about the new financial reporting systems his company had put in place, he said that he didn't use them. Instead, he explained to me that he had someone under him prepare abstracts of them for him. He explained, "I'm too old to learn how to use this stuff—and anyway, I'll be able to retire in about six years." A few months later, after the size of his staff had been dramatically reduced in a cost-cutting drive, he often found himself unable to answer questions at meetings. His far smaller staff did not always get the abstracts to him on time. Soon after, he was let go. At fifty-six he found himself looking for a job in an industry that was busily reducing costs—and facing the prospect, if he did manage to find one, of learning exactly the sort of systems he'd wanted to ignore.[16]

Continual learning also makes sense because the more skills you have, the easier it is for you to learn more—to be cross-trained. For example, if you know one foreign language, it is far easier to learn another because you know what is involved in learning a foreign language: you have learned how to learn one. The same is true of most computer programs: temporary placement agencies short of good people trained in a new word processing program will often teach it to applicants who are proficient on other programs—it represents a much smaller investment of time to pick up a new system than to learn the first one.

Continual learning is also important because as you grow older the way you learn changes. These changes are gradual, but if you haven't attempted to learn anything for decades, they can seem overwhelming and can lead you to believe you have lost the capacity to learn. Part of the problem is that courses are all too often aimed at the young. For example, theoretical training is not as easy when you get older; hands-on training tends to work better. If you have been taking courses and spent time in training programs, you realize that some parts of courses have become harder for you than they were before but that in the end you do well. You understand the need to adjust your approach to learning, and you can wait for the parts that come easier and go back and learn what you missed later. If you have not been in a learning environment since school, when you enter one with the additional stress of being unemployed, you may fail to achieve your objective. The way to avoid this is to keep on learning.

Organizational and Personal Responsibilities

Organizations must begin to assume greater responsibility for training and retraining. In today's tight labor market, more and more employers are doing just that to ensure they have the workers they need when they need them. Ray Sata sums up the reason for the growth of corporate training efforts in *Sloan Management Review*: "The rate at which individuals and organizations learn may become the only sustainable competitive advantage, especially in the knowledge intensive industries."[17]

In addition, there is "growing recognition of the importance of informal training and learning programs where training is integrated with work on the job. For example, when employees undergo on-the-job training, participate in peer training sessions or employee quality councils, or teach a training course, they are certainly learning new skills and new roles."[18] Moreover, these activities can become a normal part of work, and are not particularly costly. In fact, in today's flexible organizations, where people are brought in to do specific jobs for a short period in response to market demand, the ability of full-time employees at all levels to pass on the skills they acquired in this way is essential.

Some organizations, however, still leave formal training and development to the individual because they fear that helping employees earn advanced degrees and certificates results in their leaving for other positions. The experience of Silicon Valley—where the movement of people from one company to another has created enormous strength and growth—should help counter that fear, making it possible for you to get assistance from your current employer. If you cannot get training any other way, however, you will have to bite the bullet and find the funds, which brings us to the final action step.

Financial Planning

One of the realities of today's uncertain world is that you need to save to get through the many career shifts you are likely to make. Charles Heckscher writes in *White-Collar Blues*, "People save for their children's college education, and they may raid that fund if they are laid off; they rarely create a fund specifically for unemployment."[19] Keep in mind, however, that you need to keep a fund for more than living expenses while job hunting—you need to have enough set aside for retraining. Although there are government programs that will help with this, they are usually available only when you are unemployed, which is not the point if your goal is continual learning.

Unpleasant as it sounds, another way to keep your anxiety level low is to live below your current income. Not only does it enable you to save, it makes it far easier to switch careers, a step that often involves taking a job at a lower starting salary. Although it does not seem like much consolation to those suffering the effects of all these dislocations, in the end, the advent of these new technologies will make us all winners, improving everyone's standard of living, just as the new technologies of the industrial revolution ended up doing in England.

Let the Music Begin

Once you have accepted the fact that the changes brought by advances in information and communications technology are ongoing and you take action to be certain that you do not suffer because of them, you will find that change brings blessings as well as burdens. Life today is different, but so many of the differences clearly are beneficial, such as advances in medical technology. Other changes, of course, do not seem beneficial on an individual level for a long time. Those, as we shall see in the next chapter, are the changes that have revolutionized the world of work. They are changes whose consequences have been immediate and painful to so many, but these changes present challenges that can be overcome.

Tips for Achieving Acceptance of Constant Change

Make learning and acquiring new skills a continuing process.

- Take advantage of formal and informal training opportunities on the job.
- Continue your training and education outside work, either in courses and workshops or on your own.
- Find the learning strategies that work best for you.
- Keep abreast of technological changes and developments in your field by reading newspapers and journals and watching informational television.

Never stop building and refining your career connections.

- Keep in touch with people in your field by joining professional organizations.
- Find and join useful chat groups on the Internet.
- Keep in touch with recruiters, even when you're not looking for a job.

Focus on the concept of career—rather than just the next job.

- Assess your career and reevaluate your goals at regular intervals.
- Keep tabs on the stability (or lack of stability) of your industry, company, and department.
- Revise your résumé regularly, updating skills, experience, and objectives.
- Become a regular want ad reader, and don't limit yourself to the ads in your field.
- Make conscious decisions about the role technology will play in your career.
- Consider jobs in technology as either long-term career options or stepping-stones to new careers.

Organize your finances for a life of continuous change.

- Build a reserve fund to use during periods of unemployment or underemployment.
- Do your best to live *below* your means.
- Include funds for continuing education and training in your budget.

Chapter Four

Understanding Today's Workplace

"Would you tell me, please, which way I ought to
go from here?" asked Alice. "That depends a good
deal on where you want to get to," said the Cat.
—*Lewis Carroll*, Alice's Adventures in Wonderland

Much of the anxiety caused by technological advances is a direct
result of the downsizings and displacements that marked the late
1980s and early 1990s. The changes in organizational structure
that took place as companies turned more and more to advanced
technologies in response to globalization, a worldwide economic
downturn, and increased competition affected workers at all levels. The world of work that we all understood and were comfortable with disappeared, replaced by a world of work that seems to
value the latest skills over dedication, that provides little security
or benefits, that asks for endless hours but does not reward sacrifice
with loyalty.

To succeed in this new workplace requires new skills, new
approaches, and acceptance of new rules of employment, all of
which bring a great deal of uncertainty. In this environment, every
new development is seen as such a threat that for some the only
reaction is often a kind of paralysis, a "maybe if I don't look it will
disappear" approach. Unfortunately, that response is a road to certain failure. Success in the world of work now demands acquiring
skills quickly, interacting easily, and accepting responsibility for our
own employability.

This sounds much harsher than the reality actually feels, for the new world of work also offers opportunities for personal growth and expansion of horizons. You are no longer locked into a single set of tasks; there is no advantage to staying in a dead-end job for years to show your reliability; you can develop your own model of employment. Each of us must examine this new world of work, the downsides and the upsides, and figure out for ourselves where we want to get and the way to get there. (Note that this chapter is the main source of the answer to one of the questions asked earlier: What impact will these changes have on business and how will that affect us on a personal level?)

This step of the framework, understanding, will help you learn about the new environment created in large part by technological advances. Only then can you figure out what role you want to play in that world and what skills it will take. Making these decisions will also liberate you from your fears and allow you the freedom to learn more about how to work with and use these technologies to your advantage.

The New Corporate Landscape

As we entered the last decade of the twentieth century, "The emergence of a highly competitive global economy in which multinational corporations played a greater role; the growing importance of information as an economic resource and basis for competitive advantage; and the shift from mass production to a system of customized, flexible production" made it critical that businesses find new ways to operate.[1] In fact, as the 1980s drew to a close, businesses that once felt secure were suddenly confronted with competitors who could not only produce the same products at lower cost but could rapidly develop newer versions of their most profitable products. Driven to find new ways to compete, managers turned to technology to analyze their businesses, the ways they managed their organizations, and the processes they had in place.

Their goal was to find ways to cut costs as well as find new things to do and new ways to do them.

In the course of these reevaluations, businesses discovered ways to use technology to automate back office functions and redo processes, and they learned which things they did well and began to focus on those as well as to eliminate those that did not seem to be among their core competencies. Then, just as businesses were restructuring to take advantage of what they had learned, a global economic downturn began. The result was the avalanche of down-sizings that took place in the late 1980s and early 1990s.

This unfortunate confluence of events exacerbated the effects of the technological advances: not only were the skills needed for many jobs changing, but jobs themselves grew scarce, unemployment rose, replacement jobs were far lower paid. Corporate loyalty to employees seemed to evaporate in the face of the drive toward corporate survival: once-proud companies such as IBM and Sears were suddenly the focus of stories that asked if they were, like the dinosaurs, facing extinction. Moreover, with companies in survival mode, retraining was hard to find—and in a difficult job market, displaced workers were loath to spend what savings they had on training that might become obsolete tomorrow. One result was anxiety and anger among those who were directly affected as well as all those hearing about and knowing many who were affected.

The chaos of those years was difficult to deal with. At the height of the downsizings that brought so much anxiety to all workers, AT&T laid off some 40,000 people. Some of those who left chose early retirement, ended up taking lower-paid jobs because their skills were not saleable, or became contingent workers, moving from one short-term assignment to another.

In the half-dozen years that followed, however, AT&T—like many other companies that downsized—found itself adding to its workforce. In fact, over the following four years, AT&T hired 46,000 employees with the skills needed in the areas in which it decided to expand. It also increased the number of contracts it had with outside firms, relying on them to handle many functions previously done in-house; it brought in numerous consultants; and it used far more contract employees to help handle work in busy periods, resisting the impulse to add full-time workers.

As company after company took similar action, profits increased, raising the value of stocks. Maintaining those increased profits, however, often took repeated downsizings. "Lean and mean" was the watchword. After a while, it became clear that downsizing alone did not bring increases in profitability, and companies began to look for new ways to grow.

The search had barely begun when the global economy bounced back. This sudden turnaround showed that the new organizational forms—so painfully developed during the preceding years—were remarkably well suited for making rapid change in response to market demands. The ability to change proved the key to success in this hot new economy.

Today, many companies are engaged in work that is quite different from the work they traditionally did, and many do some of the same work but have added entirely new kinds of work based on their core competencies. Some energy companies, for example, have discovered that they really aren't very successful producers of energy. Instead, they now buy energy and use their infrastructure to deliver it to their customers; they have also entered into other kinds of work based on their relationships with their customers, such as servicing the appliances that use the energy they deliver. A major manufacturer of technological components has discovered that its methods of shipping those components around the world is the basis for becoming a logistics company. An insurance company realized that the systems it had developed to improve its customer relations division could be adapted to other companies' needs and now sets up such services for others, including a major seller of flowers by phone and some mutual fund companies.

The changes that made these companies so flexible include changes in the ways they are governed and in the ways leadership is handled. More to the point, they have changed the very nature of work for many people, just as the change from a predominantly agricultural to an industrial era did. To understand the changes that have taken place in the world of work, we first need to explore the changes that have taken place in organizational structure, leadership, and technology.

Virtually an Organization

It is important to understand the shape that organizations have been gravitating toward as well as the new conception of business processes because both affect the nature of work. In the broadest terms, the changes of the past decade have altered the shape of organizations from huge, structured hierarchies to more flexible forms that allow them to respond to market demands quickly.[2]

Of course, the flexibility in an organization depends to a large extent on the nature of its products. For example, companies involved in manufacturing have more rigid structures than service organizations. However, a company that sells a product manufactured by someone else under its auspices may be a totally flexible, even a virtual company.

The truly virtual company is usually a small enterprise that is organized by an entrepreneur, whether to provide a service or to produce a product; the company itself has no fixed core and is usually set up to fill an immediate need. It is an amalgam of people and other businesses who come together at various times. For example, the entrepreneur may have had an idea about producing a variant of a product aimed at a somewhat different market from that of the standard product in the field.

Because the market is limited and the product is seasonal, it wouldn't pay to invest in a plant for manufacturing or hire permanent staff. So the entrepreneur begins by hiring a designer to adapt the standard version of the product to the needs of the specialty consumer, then finds a plant making the standard product that can regear to make the new version. The next need is to hire someone to market it and salespeople to approach the right kinds of stores.

The business does not require a full-time accountant, and in any case our entrepreneur assumes that the companies that turn out the standard model will pick up the slightly changed version next summer and use brand recognition to put the upstart out of business, so an agency that provides accountants for short-term assignments is the obvious source for the job.

Let's assume the product is successful; the profits are good and the name the marketing group developed and promoted has caught on. The owner of the company now has a number of decisions to make: take the profits and move on, or take the profits and use them to begin to compete with the manufacturers of the original product by adding the standard versions of the product to the new product lines. This is likely to result eventually in a much more "real" company, one with offices, employees, and equipment. Or, determined not to move beyond owning a virtual company, our entrepreneur can decide to hunt for new products and develop them in much the same way as the first product and continue to build the name of the company, which will make it possible to introduce new products more easily when opportunities arise.

Maintaining a flexible company is more difficult the more products involved and the more successful the company. Because under the second and possibly even under the third scenario our entrepreneur will reach a point where one person cannot oversee all the facets of the operation alone, the company is likely to accumulate a staff, need office space to house them, and so forth. An owner who is aware of both personal strengths and company core competencies can decide where to build and how. Of course, many of these decisions run counter to the idea of the virtual company.

For example, the entrepreneur might hire designers and a few managers with particular skills in negotiation and oversight to take care of the relations with various manufacturing plants so the company never has to build its own plant. It might prove effective to enter into a long-term retainer arrangement with the marketing firm that served the company so well when it was starting out, and perhaps to bring the temporary accountant on full-time. However, instead of hiring a sales force, it may work better to hire a part-time sales manager, someone who has developed an independent sales force that can work for several companies at once.

The result is an amalgam that is very flexible. If the entrepreneur were to decide to shift products, different manufacturers could be involved and the sales force could change. In slow periods and between decisions as to what to tackle next, the marketing firm would stay on to keep the company name in the limelight, and so would a few key employees. Very few people would actually work for the company full-time, but those who did would be critical to its future and would house the institutional memory.

Of course, all of this is made possible by technology. The manufacturing plant gets copies of all incoming orders so it can decide when to gear up to produce more of the product, ensuring that the lag in time between order and delivery never goes above a predetermined time. The entrepreneur can work with the marketing group as quickly as if they were in-house because one of their employees takes a specific, continuing interest in this account and thus does not have to come up to speed before responding to its needs. Material can be sent back and forth for approval electronically most of the time, and by overnight delivery the rest. Likewise, sales meetings are usually teleconferences—which keeps costs down—and other activities are also mediated by technology rather than face-to-face interaction as much as possible.

Bending with the Wind

Another major change in the landscape is a result of the changes made by companies that started out as traditional, hierarchical organizations but then moved toward more flexible models as they adopted many of the management tools of the late 1980s and 1990s, such as activity-based costing, business process reengineering, team structures, total quality, and new technologies of various types. Many of these innovations had unintended consequences, such as the loss of institutional memory, that proved disruptive until they were better understood. A basic understanding of the changes that resulted from all of this will help further broaden your picture of the current employment landscape and make the new world of work clearer.

The large corporations of the post–World War II era thrived in an environment in which their products were in great demand after the massive war effort, which had put a premium on production aimed at meeting the needs of the military. There was a great deal of pent-up demand for new goods to replace older models of every-thing from refrigerators to furniture and to fill the new houses being built as the soldiers returned. These corporations were also benefi-ciaries of the sudden awareness of our products on the part of the citizens of many third-world countries where Americans had been stationed.

To meet this demand, American corporations focused on mass production, which meant that companies were centralized with rigid corporate hierarchies. Centralization facilitated the ordering of goods in bulk to achieve economies of scale in purchasing, allowed the close supervision of personnel, and ensured both that orders and procedures were controlled and communicated from the top to the furthest regions of the organization and that progress and problems were communicated back up to the level needed to make decisions on a corporation-wide basis. Tasks were fragmented to workers on assembly lines. Workers needed little training for their specific jobs and reported to people one step up the ladder, who in turn reported up the next step with their tallies of goods produced, worker performance, and so on. As companies grew and added more plants to facilitate output, they put in place more layers of control. Because they never lacked for customers, they did not worry too much about issues such as high inventory or duplication of steps involved in replicating the organization in other places.

When competition began to emerge here and abroad, the costs of these built-in inefficiencies took their toll. At that point, the ways in which these businesses operated began to be more carefully scrutinized. Many redundancies and inefficiencies were uncovered, often involving steps that added no value to products. If a company put technology in place that could assemble data on inventory in all its warehouses, for example, it might discover excess stock of certain products in certain regions and adjust production and shipping schedules. Management discovered that the warehousing of enormous inventories could be eliminated by producing to order. In other words, an organization spread out across the country could achieve efficiencies if it could collect, store, analyze, and share information electronically. The value of this shared information is such that in 1996, companies spent an estimated $42.5 billion worldwide to link their computers into enterprisewide systems so management could monitor finances and inventories in real time.[3]

In addition, once the technology was in place, the ability to collect information and use it for decision making eliminated many of the jobs of middle management. Then, as the notion of teamwork took hold, especially in the automobile industry, another of the responsibilities of middle management disappeared—the communication of information between groups doing specific functions that had to be coordinated.

Today, a company seeking a new design for an old product puts together a team consisting of an engineer, a designer, a market researcher, a sales manager, and an accountant. The team works together on the project for a specified amount of time. The advantages are personal interaction that allows for communication, brainstorming, and creativity that result in a product that is geared to a specific need.

If the company truly understands team-based work, the individuals assigned to the team know that part of their salary review will include the team's performance. As a result, they don't worry about spending less time on their regular assignments. The people working in such settings have no managers to explain what they are doing or how to incorporate various ideas, so they all need solid, jargon-free communications skills—after all, the engineer and sales manager must be able to speak the same language if they are to help the team achieve its goals. To complicate matters, changes such as these tend to take place in every corner of an organization at the same time.

Even those who work in major companies in the field of technology have felt the sting of the changes technology has brought. The story of IBM, which made technology a household name and was responsible in large part for the idea of lifetime employment, is a lesson in the effects of changing technology on the workplace. IBM, home of the large mainframe computers, was overtaken by the advent of personal computing in the late 1980s, when it failed to understand the strength of the technology revolution that was taking place. The problem was a combination of its huge workforce (some 400,000 workers), its massive bureaucracy and extensive sign-off procedures, and its belief that it was so strong nothing could go wrong. IBM simply continued to market its mainframe computers to a world that was seeking more flexible, less expensive systems.

The years that followed were tumultuous, resulting in a loss of some 150,000 jobs from 1990 through 1993. Finally, under Lou Gerstner, IBM remade itself by focusing on offering customers solutions rather than standardized hardware and software. Gerstner tore down the centralized bureaucracy, restructured the organization, and began hiring once again, finding people with the skills needed to remake the company. Today, IBM has a workforce of 270,000, with a small headquarters (instead of the massive buildings that once proclaimed its importance) that is itself a statement of how dramatically the company has changed.[4]

The Better to Serve You

In 1850, what is known as the *goods sector*—farming, manufacturing, construction, and mining—employed a little over 80 percent of the workforce, while the *service sector*—everything from burger flippers to brain surgeons—employed somewhat less than 20 percent. That began to change dramatically in the second half of the twentieth century, with the birth of new technologies and management improvements. Organizations became more efficient and fewer people were needed to produce goods (the very same thing that had happened in agriculture, displacing those who worked the farms). At the same time, in the booming economy of the post–World War II period, the demand for services increased. People had more to spend on everything from eating out to entertainment, the financial services industry expanded, and health care grew into a major industry. Even manufacturing companies increased their service components, adding technical support workers and departments geared to fulfilling service contracts on the products they produced. By 1996, about 75 percent of workers were employed in service sector jobs.[5]

For the most part, what the service sector provides cannot be produced in advance and then stored until a customer wants it (think of health care and transportation), the products often are intangible (an operation or a legal opinion), and most service workers deal directly with customers (the telephone sales representative or the UPS driver). Changes are taking place in this sector as well due to advances in technology: today, you can bank or buy stocks over a computer or Touch-Tone phone. What is also noteworthy is that the providers of services have various skill levels, ranging from extensive training (brain surgeon) to almost none (bedpan delivery, collection, and cleaning).

The model of work for service providers is also quite different from the model for manufacturing: part-time work is more common, work is less bound to a specific place, it often is not necessary to do it in conjunction with others, and the jobs are in general less stable. Much of the work in this sector involves the manipulation of information with the aid of technology. It also tends to involve less brawn and more brain. There is more creativity and decision making at lower levels and a greater need to communicate with others to convey information in both written and oral form.

The effects of these kinds of changes extend up into the organization, having more impact the higher up you go. It is in this area that some of the most disruptive changes in terms of work are taking place. For example, take a state agency charged with assessing property values; today, because of advances in technology, that agency may well have far fewer employees than it did twenty years ago. The first change would have come when an assessor, someone charged with checking properties on-site, was given a small, hand-held gadget with a penlike device that could be used to fill out a form that was then sent electronically to a predetermined list of recipients by pressing a button on the device instead of turning in the report on paper. Clerks were no longer needed to ensure that the forms brought in by the assessors were copied and sent to the right people. No one had to type up the information because the computer could read the numbers and automatically forward the information to the state real estate division, the tax division, and so forth.

In addition, because fewer people could handle the work, the agency needed fewer managers to supervise the direct workers— and so on up the chain of command. When it comes to work that has not changed at such a basic level—for example, bookkeeping— the difference is that the same amount of work that once took a group of people two days to do, can now, with the aid of machines, be done by a single person in a day. Again, the result is fewer em-ployees. Of course, there is now a technology group that did not exist before, so the number of employees overall has not decreased that dramatically. In other words, the change that seemed so simple is far more complex, involving displacements of various kinds.

New and Newer

Almost every change we have just looked at had its roots in the advances that were made in computer and information technology over the past thirty years. Through the early 1970s, a tour of the back office of any insurance company included a look at the finance office. An impressive array of desks lined up, one to two to three across and row upon row, filled with clerks entering payments on policies in ledgers, totaling accounts received. Another, very simi-larly configured room was occupied by women sitting in front of typewriters, preparing policies, sending out notices about missed payments, and responding to simple queries. (The contents of those letters either had been dictated to them or were preprinted on standard form letters to which they were adding addresses.)

First, the accounting function was computerized. Those rows of clerks were replaced by huge computers that stored enormous amounts of information. Connected to those central computers were terminals that could access the data in the computers and use it to do calculations in accordance with rules contained in specific applications an operator called up. The result was that one clerk could, with the aid of the computer, do the work that five or ten people had been doing by hand. The typists soon suffered the same fate as word processing programs allowed the machines to personalize hundreds of form letters in minutes, again replacing workers.

It wasn't all a story of jobs eliminated, however. The software that ran those computers had to be developed by trained accountants who could work with analysts and programmers to develop those applications. Then computers had to be bought and installed, workers trained to use them, and so forth. Perhaps it is ironic, but the fastest-growing industry today, the one creating enormous wealth as well as enormous disruptions in the nature of work, is the computer industry—and, as we shall see in Chapter Eight, it is the industry that is having the greatest problem finding people with the skill sets it needs to keep growing.

The New Look

This brief look at the new world of the flexible organization makes it clear that the world of work today is very different from what it was a decade or two ago. Looking at the problems facing the American worker, some bemoan the loss of guaranteed lifetime employment with a particular company and others the loss of the benefits that have always come with work. This response ignores an unpleasant reality. Most people have never had guaranteed lifetime employment; in fact, according to the *Economist,* job tenure in

America has not changed significantly since the 1980s, although more people are switching jobs because of layoffs than by choice.[6] The idea of lifetime employment was a result of the long-term employment of management by many large organizations from the 1950s on. For blue-collar workers, layoffs and rehiring, especially in the automobile industry, was more likely, but unions helped workers through those difficult periods. Moreover, health and pension benefits first became a part of the compensation package offered workers during World War II, when government wage controls were in effect and it was a way to compete for scarce workers during the war years.[7]

From the end of World War II to the late 1980s, however, movement from company to company tended to be a matter of taking a set of skills carefully honed in one organization to another organization in search of advancement in the same field. Those with drive and talent perfected their skills and added to them, working their way up a chosen career ladder. It was possible to aspire to be a foreman or supervisor and then a manager because over the course of the years you learned enough about how the work was done to help others learn. Today, the skills needed for any job change rapidly and management ranks are smaller.

In the new, flexible organization, the majority of jobs are not thought of as permanent positions; maintaining only a small core of full-time employees allows companies to expand or contract in response to market demand. Many positions that once were filled by full-time employees are now outsourced—often to individuals or to companies formed by individuals who once worked for that very company full-time and who are therefore considered extremely valuable suppliers. In addition, because the nature of a company's business may change, the kinds of skills needed at any given moment may change. For example, when a new method of production comes into being, sets of skills become obsolete. Advances in information and communications technology also have brought changes in where and when work can be done.

What does this mean for your future? How do you determine what to learn next? Why not simply see if you can find a job similar to the one you had and hope for the best? To answer these questions, you need to determine what kind of organization will provide you with the greatest comfort zone given the nature of work in the information age—and then make sure that the choice you make is in alignment with the stage you have reached in your work and life cycle.

The Nature of Work in the Age of the Computer

As mankind moved from the agricultural to the industrial age, the nature of work changed. Now as we move solidly into the information age, a new set of changes is under way. Those changes will affect the impact of work on our ability to control our time, the kind of energy work involves, the rules we abide by, the creativity we are encouraged to exhibit, the stability of our jobs, the rewards we receive for doing them, and our feelings of independence (see Table 4.1).

Table 4.1 Changes in the World of Work

	Agriculture	Industry	Information
Time	Natural and self-directed	Inflexible	Self-directed
Energy	Physical	Physical and mental	Mental
Management	Independent	Paternalistic	Personally chosen
Creativity and innovation	Little scope	Limited	Demanded
Job stability	High	High	Low
Rewards	Uncertain	Certain	Uncertain
Independence	High	Low	High

Time. When people worked on farms, their time was controlled to a large extent by nature. There was a season for planting and one for harvesting, cows had to be milked, chickens and pigs fed and then slaughtered at the point where they could bring the best price. Even nonfarm occupations were controlled by nature. Not only did weaving require daylight but the best time to sell the cloth was during market time, when farmers selling their crops were ready to purchase goods with their profits.

Shoshana Zuboff points out in *The Age of the Smart Machine* that "for all the bone-crushing labor demanded of the agricultural worker or the cottage weaver, the traditional rhythms of exertion and play were a world removed from the behavioral demands of industrial production. Work patterns were irregular, alternating between intense effort and idleness. Most work activities emanated from the home, and the distractions of family, the taverns, and the social web of the community limited any undivided commitment to work."[8]

Once manufacturing moved to factories and the assembly line, workers were expected to work to a given schedule. This model of work was extended to management, who had to be present when the machines were operating. The inflexibility was very troubling to those who had lived a far different life, but people adapted over time, though resentment at the loss of freedom made work something most people did because they had to. Part of the inflexibility was a way of exerting the control that was necessary in an age in which most people were engaged in manufacturing.

This is once again changing as we move to the information age. Many kinds of service work can be done on flexible schedules; creative occupations often allow people to work on projects when and where they choose, so long as a given delivery date is met. In another way, the rules of time have been broken, with projects worked on across the continent or globe on a twenty-four-hour basis.

To decide what kind of organization suits your needs, ask yourself how valuable time is to you and how self-motivated you are. Do you have other things in life that you prefer to spend time on, even if it means earning somewhat less? Do you need structure and deadlines to work efficiently? Do you like being in a given place on a routine basis? The more time means to you and the more you are self-directed, the more you fit into the newest organization forms.

Energy. The hard physical labor of the agricultural age and the steel mill and manufacturing plant has largely been supplanted by sophisticated machinery. Moreover, much of the work of the information age requires brain rather than brawn. Mental energy, not physical, is what counts. Indeed, this has been a steady development since the agricultural age, with declining amounts of personal energy expenditure being replaced first by machine energy in massive amounts—and now by computers.

Ask yourself if you can sit still in front of a computer for hours or if you prefer a great deal of activity. For example, sitting in front of a computer writing code takes a certain mind-set. Needing to expend more physical energy to be comfortable does not, however, relegate an individual to industrial age work. You might think about certain service sector jobs that allow more scope for the expenditure of physical energy. If you are someone who needs constant activity, challenges, and different environments, you might think about teaching or consulting.

Management. In the agricultural age, most people were free to manage their own plot of land the way they wanted to so long as they produced enough to feed their families and pay tax assessments or rent. They ran their farms according to traditions handed down from generation to generation. Large landowners hired workers, but these workers supplemented their incomes with what they could grow on the plots of land surrounding their cottages. Other products were manufactured and sold by independent craftsmen who were free to produce as much or as little as they wanted.

When technology improved farming and made possible the manufacture of previously handcrafted goods by machine, this all changed. Those who had the money to invest in the new equipment had specific goals in terms of the return on their investments. They laid down strict rules of control for those who worked for them so as to run their farms and plants in the most profitable way possible. Management was omnipresent, controlling every move employees made.

The arrival of advanced technologies has changed that. Work in the information age is often under far less control, in part because there is more scope for creativity and in part because of the development of different work structures such as project teams. Today, it is possible to find organizations all along the spectrum of management. In deciding what kind of organization you want to work for, ask yourself whether you like having someone explain things to you, set parameters, and take responsibility for deciding what will get done. Or would you rather be responsible for decision making— and accept the risks? Your preferences here can help you decide between companies that encourage interdependent teams and those that have moved to extremely flattened structures where individuals are given accountability and responsibility. The less you like the idea of reporting to others, the more you should think about various forms of self-employment.

Creativity and innovation. Leaving aside the truly creative professions such as music and the arts, work has rarely been a place to express creativity. Unless one was involved in a craft, there was little scope for it in the agricultural age. Breaking through tradition was a long, painstaking process taking generations. In the industrial age, the assembly line worker was no more than a pair of hands doing a specific function; as the notion of teamwork took hold, there was some scope for innovation—especially if it involved improving processes to save costs. The industrial age, however, brought more creative fields into existence—marketing and advertising, for example. As products became more and more available, design began to be important. The information age is very different; companies are open to new and creative approaches to everything from accounting to sales—if they will add value to the services and products they offer.

Some companies place high value on creativity, others are slower to do so. The kind of management in place also makes a difference. While there are older companies such as 3M that have long been known for rewarding creativity, the entrepreneurial organizations that have flourished over the past decade are the best choice if you believe you are creative and innovative. Ask yourself how important it is to you to be allowed to develop your own ideas, to be on the leading edge. The more important it is, the more likely you are to want to stay away from industrial age organizations.

Job stability. In the agricultural age, a skill learned was usable over a lifetime. In the industrial age, basic skills might have to be upgraded, but a large percentage of jobs tended to remain the same over time. Today, not only do jobs disappear, but the skills needed for some jobs change so dramatically that they might as well have disappeared. Moreover, new jobs are constantly being created as technology comes more and more into play, changing the way work is done.

The central question to ask yourself is, How risk averse are you? The more you need the comfort of knowing exactly what will happen next, the more you must strive to become part of the full-time workforce at a large organization that may be willing to retrain you as things change. Those for whom the answer is, "I'd rather learn something new than do the same thing over and over" or "I'll take the risks for the rewards," should look at the other end of the spectrum, seeking opportunities for entrepreneurship.

Rewards. The age of agriculture was an age of uncertainty when it came to financial rewards. Not only could a drought wipe out a farmer, it affected everyone in the society at the same time, so there was little in the way of a social safety net for most people. Survival was often a matter of luck; for an example, we need only look to the famines in Africa. In the industrial age, work was rewarded by paychecks, no matter how small, and in the industrial nations, social safety nets and the development of unions helped ensure survival until the next job could be found.

Today, in addition to social safety nets such as unemployment insurance, retraining opportunities are expanding as the demand for greater technological skills has increased, and it has become clear that we need them for our national economic growth. For example, the Defense Department sponsors a retraining program for aerospace engineers whose skills could translate into expertise in computers. Training is also available for those with a far less technological background. The Computer Task Group in Buffalo, which provides corporations with staffs of IT specialists, trains people from every kind of background for less sophisticated computer jobs, for example, diagnosing specific problems. These jobs, says Gail Fitzgerald, the company's director, which pay as much as $35,000 a year, have been filled by "an accountant, a lawyer, a high school literature teacher, a professor from the University of Alaska, several musicians."[9] The major difference is that the rewards of these jobs are often, especially for retrained workers, less than they were earning in the jobs that disappeared, after periods of high expense and little income during training.

The questions to ask here involve trade-offs. How much security would you trade for various kinds of satisfaction? Would you trade time with your family for a slightly lower standard of living? Would you give up financial rewards now for long-term rewards?

Independence. The transition to the information age is bringing a return to a more independent way of life. Ownership of the tools of a trade and transferable skill sets are once again enabling workers to market themselves in very different ways. Working for a large company producing a specific product limited one's options; people were pigeonholed into certain industries and certain jobs within those industries. If you worked for one of the major automobile manufacturers, airplane manufacturers were not interested in interviewing you. Today, with the rapid growth of technology, not only has a whole new field opened to all who are willing to learn, but it is far easier to go into business for yourself.

Does it matter to you if you work for yourself or for others? Is the value of the kind of work you do more important than anything else? What are your long-term goals?

Alternative Work Models

You need to think about where you are comfortable in terms of each of the characteristics we have just examined before you can decide what kind of work future you need to try to build. The first step is to ask yourself which of the following models of work best fits your decisions about where you want to be in terms of each of the characteristics.

• *Working for a large organization that has been around for a long time, where you will be responsible for imparting your skills to new employees when they are added to the workforce.* In such an organization, you will have opportunities to learn some new skills but not a lot of opportunities to advance. Salary and benefits will be steady and hours reasonable but the opportunity to accumulate wealth small.

• *Working for a large organization involved in advanced technologies or communications that is still in a growth mode.* In such an organization, there are times when people are working round the clock but receiving good salaries—with the opportunity to accumulate wealth through stock options. Working for such a company requires leading-edge skills that have to be constantly upgraded and often skill changes take place so rapidly that new employees just out of school are brought in and older ones let go.

• *Working for a smaller established company that provides services to larger companies.* This type of company provides benefits to full-time employees but tends to keep the permanent workforce small because of slow periods. Such companies do, however, use many contract workers and try to provide them with sufficient rewards so that they will return when they are needed.

• *Working for a new, entrepreneurial company geared to be a supplier for larger companies.* This type of company offers a smaller plate of benefits and the jobs are somewhat uncertain, but you can exercise a lot of flexibility on the job and the team spirit and atmosphere can be fun.

• *Working for a temporary-help company that will send you out on assignment, often long-term contract work for larger companies embarking on new product launches.* Many companies of this type act as your employer rather than merely as a contract-finding agent, providing at least minimal benefits and some guarantees of salary when times are slow.

• *Working for yourself.* Self-employment comes in many forms. You may put together a package of work of various types, perhaps a part-time job at a larger organization plus a few days a week of temporary work. You may be able to get long-term, say, two-year contracts that will guarantee some sort of training as they wind down. You may set up a business of your own with a few partners, or you may establish a virtual consulting firm that allows you to win lucrative contracts. One of the realities of this choice is that salaried workers who choose this path tend to earn less than before, but as a study of workers in Vermont laid off by General Electric showed, of the 38 percent of the workers who chose self-employment, "90 percent felt that their 'current job was better than their GE job' and hoped to remain in it."[10]

To decide which way you want to move, you must also evaluate the stage you are at in your life and work cycle. This is not a matter of age alone. Say, for example, that a fifty-five-year-old worker has two children who have completed their college educations. He owns a home and has one aged parent who is fairly comfortable, but he has little in the way of savings or pension accumulation. This man may choose to develop skills that will allow part-time work well into what would be normal retirement age. As another example, let's say that a worker just five years younger has a solid pension fund and some savings but also has three teenaged children who are going to college. This worker may decide to enhance current skills and to add some with the goal of staying with one firm for as long as possible. As a third example, say that a sixty-year-old has no children. She has solid savings and a small pension, but she is also responsible for elderly parents who are poor and in ill health. She may decide to become an entrepreneur, but she plans to do it by buying a franchise of an established firm with a couple of partners so as to ensure less risk and more freedom. Finally, let's imagine that

Tips for Understanding the New World of Work

Learn about the ways in which the world of work has changed as technology has changed.

- Ask yourself how the nature and structure of work in earlier periods differ from the nature and structure of work today.
- Consider how the nature and structure of work in earlier periods affected other aspects of people's lives.
- Find out as much as you can about what the world of work looks like today.
- Think about how recent changes in the world of work are likely to change people's lives.

Try to determine what influences your comfort level.

- Ask yourself how you react to risk and change.
- Decide what is more important to you, security or large financial rewards.
- Think about what degree of independence would make you most comfortable.
- Consider how much you care about creativity and opportunities for decision making.
- Consider the stage you have reached in your life cycle and your personal and family needs.

Decide what type of organization will provide you with the best work environment.

- Compare the characteristics of large and small, old and young, traditional and leading-edge companies.
- Ask yourself what it would be like to work at each type of company.

Decide what type of employment arrangement is best for you.

- Compare the characteristics of the different arrangements, such as being a full-time employee, temping, and being an independent contractor.
- Think about the advantages and disadvantages of each arrangement.

a forty-year-old has a wife with great earnings potential, a child whose grandparents have put aside enough for a college education, and a house inherited from an aunt. This man may decide to spend five years taking risks by starting a consulting business in a highly competitive creative area.

Conclusion

Understanding today's flexible organizations and how they are structured and operate is a critical step in mastering the anxiety caused by the effects of technology on the world of work. Once you accept that more change is inevitable and understand the new organizational structures, it will be far easier to anticipate further developments. You now have a context in which to examine trends and developments. The tools for this examination are presented in the next step of the framework—gathering and analyzing information to establish a knowledge base for decision making about your future in the continually changing world of work.

Chapter Five

Gathering Knowledge from the Garden of Past Events

It is not enough to collect information; we must
absorb it, internalize it, and connect it to concepts
we already understand, thus making what we learn
our own before we use it.

—*Frank K. Sonnenberg*[1]

The third step of the framework involves gathering information and learning to analyze it so that you reduce the element of surprise in your life. By now, you know change is always on the horizon, and you have enough of an understanding of the new world of work to see the impact that additional changes, especially in technology, may have on that world. This step will explain how to put in context news about innovations and advances in science and technology. It will teach you new ways of thinking about what you hear and see happening in the world around you so that you can anticipate any effects they may have on the world of work. The goal is to help you decide when to retrain for your current career and whether or not to think about developing a new one.

Remember the seven questions? This chapter not only explores past developments as a means of laying out ways to analyze new developments but it also presents a detailed analysis of the development of the advanced technologies that are causing so much anxiety. The discussion will answer the first of those questions: What is the nature of the new technologies?

Learning from the Past

The relentless march of new technologies cannot be slowed. If we look back, it is clear that human curiosity and inventiveness are unbounded. From taming fire and inventing the wheel through the metalworking of the bronze and then the iron ages and to the inventions of the modern day, people have found ways to make their lives more comfortable and safer. People also have found ways to communicate better with one another, from words spoken to pictures drawn to words recorded on stone, papyrus, paper, electronic media.

Each development brought changes in the way people lived their lives. Overall, we perceive these changes to have improved the lot of mankind, and we recognize that they also brought changes in power and wealth. Another basic fact seems to be that changes that have dramatic effects on the way we live are less the result of single discoveries than clusters of innovations that build on one another. The first steps, by themselves, do not change our lives.

The other important thing to keep in mind when looking back is that just because a great change is a result of the cumulative effects of many changes does not mean it is easier to foresee. As Henri-Jean Martin writes:

> Few businessmen in the 19th century were aware of how fundamentally machinery, transportation, electricity, and communications technologies would change their lives. Most people could not foresee the profound social changes that these technologies would bring—the shift from an agricultural to an industrial-based economy; the exodus of people from rural communities to urban areas; the transformation of work from craft production to mass production; and the decline of small, proprietary business in favor of large, vertically integrated firms. Although revolutionary in their ultimate effect, the changes wrought by the new technologies took place in an evolutionary fashion. Moreover, these impacts were both positive and negative, requiring considerable time and social and economic restructuring before they could be absorbed.[2]

What we learn from studying the past then is that we cannot foresee the future with any degree of clarity. What we also learn is that change is often the result of clusters of developments; it has both good and bad effects (especially when it comes to each individual); it does not make everything in the past obsolete; and it requires a great deal of change on the part of people, organizations, and institutions. This knowledge should offer some comfort. It means that every invention we hear about is not, by itself, likely to create massive disruptions. We need to take the information and put it in context. We need to ask ourselves how a development fits with other changes, how far it will move a given area along, and what side effects it will have (that is, unintended consequences, which will be explored later).

Learning to explore new developments through comparisons and analogies with changes that have taken place in the past will make them far less worrisome. The more we think about the possible effects of an innovation, the less likely we are to feel totally overwhelmed by the actual changes it brings.

The Art of Speculation

Spending time thinking about the various consequences of developments helps in your fight to accept change as inevitable. For example, the invention of, say, the wheel made a huge difference. What if the wheel had not been invented? Without the wheel, would we have trains or cars? Well, we might have something that performed the same function, but it is unlikely we would have cars or trains as we know them. Human history might well have developed in quite a different way. For example, would we have a world totally dependent on water and boats for transportation across distances? What would that world look like? How much of the United States would be settled? Would the world be laced with canals instead of roads?

This kind of speculation is at the heart of science fiction, where authors create worlds based on the probable effects of slight changes in the world as we know it. It does not take long to see what a huge impact an invention such as the wheel had on our history. But what about smaller inventions? What would a world without elevators look like? Although seen as just a convenience when first invented, elevators made possible high-rise buildings—and our densely populated vertical cities. Or the modern refrigeration methods developed to keep perishable foodstuffs safe until use, which led to air-conditioning, which encouraged many who preferred warmer climates to settle in areas that at certain times of the year are very hot—and dry. In turn, this raised the problem of water scarcity.

Another thing to keep in mind is time. How long was it between the invention of the wheel and major developments in transportation? Does something else have to happen for an invention to have a major impact on the world? What other advances need to take place at the same time? These are the types of questions that will prove very useful when applied to your work, and they are exactly the types of questions you need to ask when thinking about the possible success of a new product.

Looking at things from different perspectives—and keeping in mind when contemplating the effects of something new that the consequences may be both unintended and contradictory—can be extremely valuable. It can lead to insights about the way the world works and teach you not to take things for granted. Consider the introduction of computers into the workplace: the new machines made some employees less valuable—middle managers, for example, were no longer needed as conveyors of commands and information. Meanwhile the same technology made others more valuable—and not just those who were building the technology, either; telephone service representatives, for example, could use their new access to detailed information both about their company's products and about individual customers to build both sales and satisfaction.

The more you look at things from different perspectives in the effort to foresee the kinds of changes that further technological advances may have, the more you gain. The effort not only prepares you for change, it accustoms you to the kind of wide-ranging thought processes that today's workplaces demand. Businesses that encourage this kind of thinking also gain tremendous advantages, as employees who are innovative and open to change can cope with a changing environment long before any central planning office could analyze their situation and reach them with guidance.

Looking Back

A good way to gain insights to the kinds of changes to watch for and the repercussions they have is to look back at various aspects of some earlier advances. The kinds of information presented about each of the developments examined vary both in order to make clear how many ways there are to look at innovations and to lay the groundwork for looking at some of the changes currently under way.

Collecting and Preserving Information

When writing first began to replace the oral tradition, people gained the ability to collect information that could be depended upon to remain the same over time. Laws could be set in stone, the events of the past could be recorded, and cultures could be preserved.

When it comes to culture, though, there are many who would argue that while writing meant that the history of a culture could be preserved forever, the loss of the oral tradition actually destroyed the culture. When it was no longer necessary to come together to hear the words of a storyteller there were fewer such group gatherings, weakening people's attachment to community. When a written communication could be perused in solitude, the sense of shared life lessened. Moreover, many would argue, community ties weaken when members are exposed to other customs and beliefs, some of which they choose to adopt.

The change from spoken to written histories was slow. The number of individuals who acquired the skills needed to participate was limited by the necessity of devoting endless hours to simply sustaining life. Thus it took a long time for literacy to spread in Western societies, and even when it did, the oral tradition never quite disappeared, continuing in the form of music, particularly folk songs, and storytelling to children.

Only those with leisure and money, which meant large land-holders or the clergy, had the time to learn to read and write. As a result, those skills became the mark of the elite of society.[3] The painstaking work involved in producing copies of written material limited their availability and also kept their costs high, further slow-ing the spread of literacy—and opportunity for advancement.

When Johannes Gutenberg moved the art of printing to a new level in the middle of the fifteenth century, an enormous change was set in motion. The speed with which these new methods spread was startling, according to Elizabeth Eisenstein, who has devoted years to the study of the effects of the printing press: "In a few decades, printers' workshops were established in urban centers throughout Europe. By 1500 various effects produced by the output of printed materials were already being registered."[4]

Once books were available in multiple copies, information could be spread to the farthest reaches of civilization. Of course, the spread of books was slowed by the limited transportation and the expense of shipping. If not for the almost simultaneous devel-opment of canals, the opening of new trade routes, and a postal sys-tem, how long might it have taken for printing to make a difference? These are the very issues that have to be addressed when deciding whether or not to build a plant in a foreign country: Is ade-quate transportation available, a literate workforce, and so forth?

Gutenberg's invention also brought about new careers. As more and more books became available, more and more libraries were set up and librarianship became a career; printing become a major occupation, and so did papermaking and bookbinding; bookstores appeared in major cities and even smaller towns. In addition, as more and more people wanted access to this tool of a better life, there was an increase in the demand for schooling, and slowly the idea of public education took hold as literacy became more and more of a necessity for getting work done.

The effects of major changes such as the development of printing are often the subject of debate. For example, some believe that the ease of spreading new ideas made the Protestant Reformation possible; others argue that the standardization of the printed liturgy sustained the broad reach and power of the Catholic church. Of course, much more could be said about the effects of printing. The points made here have been selected because they have parallels to the effects on our lives—personal, professional, and civic—of the technology that marks the emergence of the information age.

The Movement of Information

For some purposes, information must not only be recorded, it must be conveyed quickly to be of value. During the Napoleonic Wars, for example, the collecting and transfer of information on troop movements was raised to high art, with spies crossing the English Channel with information—and often contraband. Nathan Rothschild, a London financier who helped the British cause by smuggling funds across the channel to the Duke of Wellington, developed a system using carrier pigeons to convey information rapidly, and he put this information to private as well as public use. Knowing of Napoleon's defeat at the battle of Waterloo before the news was generally available, Rothschild sold government bonds short while the failure to hear of a victory was making everyone nervous and causing the market to plunge. Then he was able to buy back the bonds at distressed prices before the news broke and sent prices soaring again, redoubling his investment many times over.

The twentieth century has taken us far beyond carrier pigeons, but the essential impact of communications hasn't changed. John Brooks—a longtime contributor to the *New Yorker*—wrote, "By bringing about a quantum leap in the speed and ease with which information moves from place to place, it has greatly accelerated the rate of scientific and technological change and growth in industry."[5] But what was "it"? Not the Internet—Brooks was describing the telephone. His observation is, however, just as accurate a statement whether applied to the telephone or to the pigeon or the telegraph or the new telecommunications.

Developments that advance our ability to collect and disseminate information bring dramatic social and economic changes. One of the most dramatic effects of the telephone took place in the world of finance, the same world that Rothschild did so well in by creating a personal communication system. The stock market, formerly limited to those who congregated in the financial centers of a few large cities, was suddenly available to anyone in the country with access to a telephone. Wall Street, according to Brooks, "went national. The economic effect was to increase the liquidity of securities and to increase vastly the fund-raising capability of businesses, paving the way for economic expansion."[6]

The telephone brought numerous other changes over time, most unexpected even by those involved in establishing telephone companies. Those who first entered the business saw the telephone primarily as a business tool, something that would save time, enhance sales by making it possible to call ahead for appointments, and relay sudden orders quickly. It would also make leisure travel feasible for officers and managers by allowing employees to reach them in an emergency.

As soon as lines reached beyond cities and towns to more rural areas, however, the telephone's residential uses emerged, perhaps most notably for socializing where the distance between homes was extensive and time scarce. The phone also proved valuable for such purposes as notification of deliveries of goods or delays in getting somewhere, and summoning help in the case of emergencies. Of course, bringing telephones to these communities was slowed by the expense involved in stringing the lines across those miles of empty space.

One aspect of the development of the telephone is particularly worth noting here as we look to the past to help us understand our own age. The growth of telephone usage was not the same in homes as in businesses. Claude Fischer, who has examined the history the telephone in great detail, notes that only about 40 percent of American households had telephones in the early 1940s, and near-universal telephone service wasn't achieved until the early 1980s.[7] Contrast that with television, introduced for home use in 1945 and exceeding telephone penetration only a dozen years later. A similar pattern can be observed with an earlier innovation: in 1930, the radio (introduced in 1920) and the telephone could each be found in close to 40 percent of households; by 1935, the radio was in 60 percent of households, but telephones had gained no additional ground.[8]

Why was the telephone so slow to gain acceptance, especially for home use? And why has there never been strong demand for the videophone, which was has been available for decades? (In the past few years, videophones have gained ground as some businesses began to use them, primarily to reduce travel.) Does it have to do with notions of privacy? Does it have something to do with active and passive use? Then there is the role of cost. Fifteen years ago, one could have said that the difference between the rapid acceptance of the telephone and radio and television was cost; telephone use involved recurring costs, while radio and television were onetime purchases. But the spread of cable television has not been slowed because of recurring costs.

As noted, when it came to business, the telephone had a different history; it was rapidly adopted as a means of increasing efficiency because of the time it could save in conducting transactions. An unintended consequence was opening the workforce to women, who were believed to have more of the characteristics needed to make good telephone operators. And, of course, there were predictions that never became reality, such as the creation of a single dialect as people across different regions communicated with one another.

The Right Mix—Information, a Little; Entertainment, a Lot

As noted, in contrast to the telephone, radio and then television were adopted with incredible speed. Did that happen because they provided entertainment? Was it ease of use—neither requires learning anything—and escapism that spurred their rapid acceptance? Trying to answer questions such as these is useful preparation for determining what effects new developments that are a result of the convergence of entertainment and communications and information technology are likely to have.

Some of the benefits of the telephone, radio, and television seem similar at first glance. They all make it possible to acquire information about breaking news. Except for personal information, say, about family members (which could be brought by local telegraph office messengers almost as easily as by telephone), the radio and television are much more useful as sources of information. They allow everyone in the nation to know what is happening in any little corner of the nation and the world—and bring that information to us in the form of the actual words (and in the case of television, pictures) of respected observers or the people involved. The radio helped unite us as a nation through reports of battles in World War I and through Fireside Chats during the Great Depression. However, radio and television, much as print, also expose people to new and different ideas, including many that create dissension.

In terms of culture, these inventions created a common frame of reference for all citizens; everyone knew who Lucy was, we all knew what to wear by looking at what characters our age wore, and we knew what was "in" and what was "out." The big TV networks set our standards for us. With the advent of multichannel cable and satellite networks, that homogeneity has been threatened. Critics bemoan the fragmentation of society they believe will result from this change. Advocates point to the new social communities that develop because isolated individuals can connect with one another across continents by phone or computer, creating pockets of affinity that have little regard for time or place.

Changes in the Production and Movement of Goods

When looking at the major technological advances in the area of information collection and communication, remember that a number of other advances took place at about the same time that made those developments possible. Indeed, technological advances often build on one another. Think for a moment about the first step in using the television—plugging it into an outlet. A whole world of innovation went into the establishment of the electrical grid we take for granted today. Think about the ships and railroads that brought books and other printed materials as well as the presses for producing them to distant locations and then think of the need for steel for the steam engines, hulls, rolling stock, and tracks to make it all happen. And remember that the faster information about a new development reaches others, the faster the next development will come.

Keeping that in mind, let's turn now to some advances that affected the way people lived and the way goods were produced and distributed that were all part of the changes that brought about the industrial age.

Sources of Energy

The invention of the steam engine in 1769 by James Watt traditionally marks the start of the industrial revolution. It improved mining by helping drain deep tunnels and bring up ore in large amounts, and it improved transportation by making possible steam locomotives (1804) and steamboats (1807). Again, however, exploring this period makes clear that a single invention does not revolutionize the world. The improvements in mining helped increase the production of the coal needed for the making of iron and steel to build the rails, and so forth. In 1855, Henry Bessemer developed the process that improved steel production, reducing costs and improving quality. Then Edwin Laurentine Drake came along in 1859 looking for a better fuel for lamps than coal, and petroleum was on its way to becoming the fuel of choice. With gasoline available, the internal combustion engine became possible (Etienne Lenoir, 1862), and in about thirty years, we had the Model T Ford. The popularity of the Model T had unintentional consequences—the spread of the assembly line into all sorts of manufacturing operations.

Intertwined with all these advances was the development of electric power. Again, we have a cascade of interrelated innovations from people working in the same area, learning from what they heard and read about one another's inventions:

- *Alessandro Volta*, whose connection with electricity is immortalized in the word *volt*, published his findings about the generation of electric current in 1800.
- *Hans Christian Oersted* and *André-Marie Ampère* (again someone immortalized in a name, ampere, or amp for short) showed that electric current produces a magnetic field.
- *Michael Faraday* invented the induction ring (1831) that made the generator possible.
- *Joseph Henry* invented the electric motor the same year.
- *Thomas A. Edison* invented the electric light in 1879.
- *Nikola Tesla*, a Serbian immigrant, developed alternating current while working in the United States for George Westinghouse in 1884.
- *Charles Parsons* developed, also in 1884 but in England, the steam turbine engine.

There were dozens of others who contributed to the development of usable electric power, which brought light that allowed us to work easily after dark and provided reliable power to the machines that produced the goods that changed our standard of living.

As with all other developments, the effects of these changes were often contradictory and unintended, and they did not all occur simultaneously. Indeed, changing the world is usually a slow process; for example, electric wires crisscrossed the streets of lower Manhattan and other areas where business and residences were tightly clustered early in the century but did not reach deep into rural America until the close of the decade that marked the end of World War II.

As industrialization spread, it displaced many individual workers, but over time it raised everyone's standard of living, including that of the displaced. The massive technological breakthroughs brought manufacturing into being—and urbanization. Don't forget that farm laborers fled to the overcrowded, filthy cities to find work. The cities were growing to accommodate the needs of manufacturing under the new technology, and the farm laborers were unemployed because technological advances had also occurred in agriculture, eliminating their jobs.

In fact, about 75 percent of the population was engaged in agriculture at the height of that age. At the height of the industrial age, as the number of farmworkers decreased and service industries started growing, the number of people engaged in manufacturing reached 75 percent. Today, 75 percent of the population is engaged in the service sector. Whether that means that we are in the midst of the information age and about to switch again or not is open to question. What is not open to question is the technological advance at the root of this shift.

The Computer Comes of Age

The industrial revolution laid the groundwork for the coming of the information age, the symbol of which is the personal computer. Computers were, like electricity, the result of a constant cascade of innovations. The technology moved from Blaise Pascal's 1642 computing machine (which automatically added numbers when the user moved its dials) to Gottfried Wilhelm von Leibniz's machine (with gears that shifted to allow multiplication in the 1670s) to Charles Babbage's work (which brought about, in 1812, the first model of a modern computer, using steam power to calculate and print out tables).

With the advent of electricity, punch card machines for business, scientific, and engineering calculations became practical. This early form of computing prevailed until the 1930s. Then Alan Turing created an "intelligent" machine, one that had within it rules controlling its behavior when applied to information entered into the system. World War II brought the development of far more sophisticated machines aimed at helping support the war effort by calculating ballistic tables. The most notable of those machines, ENIAC—for Electrical Numerical Integrator And Calculator—used almost 20,000 vacuum tubes and occupied almost 2,000 square feet. (Although it was considered state-of-the-art then, its work can be done today by a handheld calculator.)

Right after the war, John Von Neumann, a mathematician, developed ways to store programs (that is, sequences of coded instructions) on these machines in a format that allowed them to be modified while operational. This was the first step on the road to the creation of software as we know it today. The programs we use that allow the computer to do so many things, from word processing to playing games, would all be impossible if Turing and the people who followed had not been able to make a machine progress through logical steps on its own.

The massive machines known as mainframes were introduced by IBM in 1951; they were compatible with the punch card systems already in use. The computer was, at this stage, used primarily by scientists and scholars to handle data. Many of the earliest uses involved calculations, and computers entered the business world through finance departments.

The pattern of constant advances did not slow from that point on. Transistors began to replace the vacuum tubes and other large components of the mainframe, reducing their size. Integrated circuits appeared, allowing speedier performance. Miniaturization began—and is still at the forefront of new advances. Computer languages were developed and replaced by newer computer languages, another field that continues to flourish today. Then came the development of the personal computer in 1968, which marked the beginning of the shift from the computer as a massive number cruncher to the tiny and versatile machines many of us interact with every day.

In the mid-1970s, everything began to change. Operating systems—the enormously complex programs that direct the operation of computers and the applications that run on them—and programming languages were developed, followed by applications that could handle specific business functions such as invoicing and word processing. At the same time, many computer experts were focusing on developing a graphical user interface, which would allow users to communicate with their computers through pictures rather than words and numbers. More specifically, a graphical user interface "displays a user's options in the form of graphic images, termed icons, to which the user points using a mouse, a palm-sized device attached to the computer, the movement of which corresponds to the movement of a cursor on screen. The user selects an option by moving the mouse to position the cursor over it and pressing a button on top of, or 'clicking,' the mouse."[9]

If you found this definition not only useful but comforting, you need to begin to read some more about technology. You should learn as much as you need to be comfortable when you decide to use these machines seriously. Do you need to understand in depth what each of these developments involved and what each term means? Well, think over the review of the developments that went into the invention of usable electric power—how much of that did you know? Is knowing it important to turning on a light or plugging in a small appliance? And today, computers are far simpler to use. When it comes to business, you need to understand how to use the applications that are important to your job first. Anything else you learn is to enhance your general knowledge and help you prepare for change.

"We're All Connected"

At the moment, getting connected is what it's all about in the world of computers. Today, the computer and communications technology have converged; indeed, convergence is now considered the most important advance, the one that may change the face of the world yet again. Convergence is considered so important because it "takes advantage of the fact that data in all its forms— text, video, audio, graphics—can be turned into the language of binary arithmetic [a series of numbers that are the basis of the digital system that is used in programming] for shipment across the Net. [The Internet, which is explained in the list that follows.] For example, the telephone company . . . can acquire movies and feed them to your home through the networks it is revamping with fiber-optic connections."[10]

This enhanced form of computing may prove far more appealing because it can also be used for entertainment, for culling information from all the other computers and databases connected to it for the purpose of sharing information, reading magazines, playing games, making reservations, and even buying goods and services.

Despite the exponential growth of things you can do via a connected computer, computers are not in every home or even every office—yet. For many, there is still much about this device that is mysterious. To start the process of gathering knowledge about it, here are a few questions that always seem to be asked when the subject of getting on-line comes up in a discussion.

• *What is the "Information Superhighway" that Vice President Al Gore had everyone talking about a few years ago?* Broadly speaking, it means the Internet, which is neither a specific place nor a computer. Rather it is the network of pathways that information is transmitted on, linking all the connected machines throughout the globe together.

• *Who owns the Internet?* No one owns it. The Internet is not a thing that can be owned by a company or even a government. It is rather the links between willing individuals, companies, and governments all over the world. Everyone with the necessary equipment can connect or disconnect from the network at will.

Think of the Internet the same way you think of radio signals. Anyone can produce a signal and transmit it. Anyone else who wants to listen simply needs the equipment (the radio) and the connection (the radio frequency). Your computer is the equipment and a modem makes the connection. A *modem* is a device, either separate from and plugged into or built into your computer, that modulates the digital signal from your computer into the analog signal the telephone it is plugged into accepts. Of course, there's one big difference between the airwaves and the Internet—the government *owns* the airwaves in the name of the public and licenses the use of specific broadcast frequencies. If you try to transmit a signal without a license, you can get into serious trouble. The Internet, by contrast, is truly free—at least at the moment. Anyone really can say anything on the Net where anyone else can read it, though the feasibility and desirability of limiting that freedom are currently matters of heated debate.

- *Who built it?* It began in the mid-1960s when the U.S. Department of Defense's Advanced Research Projects Agency (ARPA) sponsored research aimed at linking computers used by scientists at research centers. The goal was to develop a series of rules (protocols) that would allow computers to communicate with one another so scientists and researchers could easily share information across geographically dispersed areas. Known as ARPANET, this network served as the Department of Defense computer network until the early 1980s. At that point it was divided into MILNET (which was to serve the needs of the military) and ARPANET (which was to serve the needs of researchers). In 1982, the network of computers involved began to expand rapidly, and the name Internet was first used to describe it.

- *How are these computers connected?* Unlike radio signals, the information on the Internet doesn't travel through the air, but rather through the same cables that your telephone signal does. Your modem translates the data into usable information from those annoying squeals you hear—in much the same way that a fax machine, using the same telephone line, can translate a document into noise and back again.

• *How does one get connected?* There are a number of ways to connect to the Internet or to a computer in your company's branch office. Most individuals use modems attached to a single phone line and an Internet device, such as a computer. Today, since so many people are interested in connecting, companies are developing "net boxes," computers that come equipped with a modem and just enough memory and software to allow you to access the Internet. These would theoretically sell for as little as $500, about half what it now costs to buy a basic computer with general applications such as word processing and spreadsheet software. However, with the expanding role of the Internet in business, it is likely that more and more people will connect through their existing computers.

There are many ways of accessing the wealth of information on the Internet—you just have to decide what best suits your needs. To gain access to the information zipping around those pathways—or even to get e-mail and send it—you need hardware and software that can filter the information coming off those digital pathways into a form you can understand and work with. There are dozens upon dozens of machines (called routers and servers) and software packages (Eudora, Netscape, America Online) that will do the translating and filtering for you.

Many large corporations have set up their own connections, buying tens of thousands of dollars worth of machinery to allow them to get all their workers on-line at minimal cost per user. That cost includes their own domain names, those strange addresses you see in so many advertisements, such as *http://www.apple.com* or *http://www.amazon.com*. A domain name is an identifying tag (like a telephone number) that servers use to route information to and from users. However, for the individual user, the most cost-efficient thing to do is to rent a part of someone else's system and name. Indeed, thousands of Internet service providers have sprung up over the past five years whose goal is to earn money by helping individuals access the Internet.

Moreover, as interest in getting connected increases, so does the range of products and companies trying to help people get on-line. Incorporating Internet software into other products is said to be the wave of the future. From televisions that can be used not only to order any movie you want to see instantly but to get your e-mail as well to computers that will allow you to do your banking and watch television while you use the Internet, integration is the key. It is seen as the next step in the evolution of the computer from a passive tool to an invaluable part of every office and household.

What's Next?

Today the Internet (of which the World Wide Web is a part) combines computing, telecommunications, information services, broadcasting, publishing, and commerce and is already having major effects. Once again, these effects are clearest in the world of finance. Walter Wriston, former chief executive officer of Citibank, says that "a brand new international monetary system has been created. Unlike all prior arrangements, this new international system was . . . created by technology. . . . [It] is not a place on a map; it is more than 200,000 monitors in trading rooms all over the world that are linked together. With this new technology no one is really in control. Rather, everyone is in control through a kind of global plebiscite on the monetary and fiscal policies of the governments issuing currency."[11]

Not everyone agrees that this global system is securely in place, however. Writing in *World Watch*, University of Virginia historian Ed Ayers says that "there is a popular impression, among the affluent and well-connected, that the global economy is now almost complete and almost everyone is a part of it. Transactions span the globe in seconds; people in the remotest corners of the world watch the TV advertising of multinational corporations; your VISA card is accepted in 224 countries and territories; and the international community, through agencies ranging from the World Trade Organization to Interpol, has become highly adept at both protecting economic activities and keeping them accountable. But that impression—of a powerfully and securely interfaced international system that now keeps track of us all—is a myth."[12]

If that is a myth, what is fact? The areas in which the effects of this global system are most clearly visible are business and the economy. To date, it has had far less of an effect on our personal and civic lives.

In terms of our personal lives, we may want but do not need this new technology at home. It is, like the telephone, a matter of choice. While some people have chosen to jump in totally, the number of those who have is not nearly as large as the forecasts by the devotees of this new form of communications thought they would be. Not everyone is on-line. Many people who have personal computers and use them choose not to connect. The huge amounts of money expected as a result of "electronic commerce" are coming from business-to-business commerce rather than business-to-consumer use. When it comes to our civic life, we still have paper ballots in some places—and no one is voting on-line. Most of our government officials, however, can be reached on-line.

The history we have explored indicates that personal use may expand the more the entertainment portion expands, but nothing, as we have seen, is that simple. The changes that the information age has made in the world of work may have vast effects on the way we live our lives, including the way we choose to spend our leisure time. For example, the less physical energy we expend at work the more we may choose more active leisure pursuits. Again, figuring out what might take place in the future is a matter of examining change in the right context and asking the right questions as we search for what is on the horizon.

Each time you become aware of a cluster of developments, start to prepare for their possible effects by asking yourself—and personal and professional friends who seem open to this kind of speculation—questions such as:

- Is this cluster of developments likely to result in major changes?
- What kinds of changes could they bring?
- What effects could those kinds of changes have on the way we live our lives?
- What effects could those kinds of changes have on the way businesses run and the work that they do?
- What kinds of work could they affect?
- If these changes came about, who would benefit, who would lose? In what ways?

Now do a little reverse engineering. When changes take place that you did not expect, ask yourself what could you have done so you would have noticed? All of this keeps you mentally alert, expands your horizons, and makes you less fearful. Try it. You are likely to come up with some scenarios that are so unpleasant that the reality will seem tame by comparison.

A Final Word

The goal of this, the third step in the framework, was to help you open yourself to knowledge and to give you a context for exploring future changes. These skills should relieve your anxiety enough to let you take the next three steps, action steps that will not only help you overcome your anxiety about technological advances but also bring you success.

The next three chapters turn from understanding to action, starting with helping you use the electronic networks that have become a critical part of the new world of work to augment the personal networking you have always done as well as support new forms of networking. Then we will explore ways to build trust in this world so as to make your networks work, and move on to ways to acquire the new skills needed for success.

Tips for Gathering Knowledge

Watch for new developments and compare them with past innovations.

- Learn about the ways in which earlier innovations changed people's lives. Think also about the aspects of life they did not change.

- Study the kinds of changes that were anticipated when a new development was announced, and then what actually happened, especially unintended consequences.

- Consider the amount of time it took after a discovery for changes to actually take place.

- Look at other factors besides the new technology that were needed for a change to occur.

- Remember that changes do not often happen as a result of a single advance, so be particularly alert to clusters of advances.

Spend time imagining the changes new developments might bring—and keep a record of your predictions.

- Consider the broader economic and social effects a development might have.

- After a new development you spent some time evaluating is in use, review your ideas about what changes it would bring.

Think about the effects these changes could have on your life.

- Stay alert for ways that knowledge about the nature of a development may help you achieve positive and avoid negative effects. (For example, understanding the vocabulary associated with a new development will make it easier to follow its progress and take advantage of it.)

- Open yourself to learning the rudiments of technology so you will be less anxious if you have to acquire specific skills.

- As you go through this process, remember that spending time learning how to deal with the effects of change, no matter how much you are stretched for time, is likely to help you avoid negative consequences.

Chapter Six

Networking

Making Critical Connections

The quantum organization will have infrastructures
that encourage and build on relationships,
relationships between leaders and employees,
between employees and their colleagues, between
divisions and functional groups, between structures
themselves.

—*Danah Zohar*[1]

Now that you understand the new world of work and how to watch
for additional changes in it, you are ready to take the next step in
the framework, finding ways to handle the critical connections with
people with whom you work, often only electronically. This is the
networking of the new world of work, a somewhat different form of
networking from what most of us think of when we hear that word.

Traditional networking involves the creation of groups of individuals with whom you have relationships of various kinds built
over time. You feel free to call upon the people in these groups,
your network, to collect information on what is happening in your
industry and your area of expertise, to look for ideas about how to
handle a project or for leads about a new job, and to determine
which organizations and individuals are most likely to be trustworthy. Traditional networking, which is personal even though it
frequently involves people met at or through work, usually involves
picking up the phone and chatting with members of the group. The
only difference that new technologies make here is that they offer
new tools for such communication—e-mail or chat groups.

Now, however, a new form of networking has developed as a result of the way organizations are structured today. This form of networking involves interacting with people you have never met but nonetheless need to work with to do your job, whether because you are assigned to a team, have to deal with alliance partners or outsourcers, or manage groups of at-home workers. This form of networking is critical to success in the new world of work. It means that you have to learn to build relationships with people in real time, often before meeting them face to face. Your traditional networks can be helpful in providing you with information about the companies and people with whom you will be working in this new way that will increase your comfort level. There are also behaviors and rules of etiquette that can smooth relations when communicating electronically.

Not only is the new networking a very effective and efficient workplace tool, it often results in relationships that add to your traditional networks. It is both a result of and enabled by the advanced information and communications systems that connect us to one another, allowing us to work together in real time, to collect and analyze information rapidly, and to work far more flexibly than ever before. While you must learn how to connect—that is, how to use your e-mail system and how to access the Internet—to network in the new world of work, you do not need to know how these systems connect.

In the course of guiding you through this step of the framework, the chapter also provides answers to another of the questions we have been exploring: How will the changes brought by these technologies affect our relationships with others? But before we go on to examine the specifics of building and managing traditional and new networks, let's stop and watch networking in action.

Extending Our Reach

Almost everyone has an anecdote proving that there are only six degrees of separation between any two individuals, and that therefore it is possible to get any information you need by making some magic (small) number of phone calls. The speed with which you can obtain such information, however, actually depends on the world in which you network.

If you are a professor of music seeking a peer to provide some information for a chapter you have written on the music of the American Revolution and its effects on public opinion in that period, you could probably track down an expert in that area with very few phone calls. You might call someone you know in the history department who tells you that the expert in the field is at a different university and that he doesn't know him personally. However, he explains, he can give you the number of someone he knows in another department at that university who might be helpful. You call that person, explain how you got her name, and ask her for an introduction to the professor you are trying to reach. She provides the number, saying, "Of course, use my name—any friend of Bob's. . . ." And so, three phone calls later, you are connected to the person who provides you with the information you need.

Why is this chain of actions described as networking? To start, remember that the first call was to someone you knew in your own school's history department. There are any number of people in that department, but when the question arose you thought of someone to whom you were somehow connected. You might have met at a faculty meeting or served together on a committee. That first meeting generated some discussion that let you know a bit about the person; a later casual encounter might have resulted in a conversation over a cup of coffee in the faculty lounge, which provided more information about the person's area of expertise, a problem with a mutual student, something that made a tie between the two of you.

All you might do at this point is exchange greetings when you pass one another and converse when at the same event, but you know from other people on campus who stop by when you are chatting, or from remarks made by people who see you with that person, that he is well regarded. When you think history, his name occurs to you and you feel free to call and ask the favor, because you assume that he'd feel free to call you if he needed to know something in your field. In other words, a connection and a degree of trust have developed between you. When he does call some weeks later with a question, you help him make a connection that will provide him with what he needs.

Of course, the fact that your request relates to expertise in a world you both inhabit cuts the number of calls it takes to get your answer by networking. If you were a journalist trying to check a single fact about a piece of music used during the revolution, it would take a few more calls, and if you were a dancer who loved doing crossword puzzles and needed that piece of information, it would probably take a larger number of calls. Your success is not merely a matter of having networks—lines of easy access between you and a group of other people to whom you are connected—but of the size, nature, and purpose of the networks to which you belong.

Electronic networking works somewhat differently. Once you know your way around that world, you can send out a simple query through a number of groups organized especially for that purpose; for example, there is a service called ProfNet—a collaborative of some five thousand public relations executives at major colleges, universities, think tanks, corporations, medical centers, and public relations firms—that is used by journalists and authors in need of information. When queries are posted, the members try to find someone in their organizations to answer them. Not only is it a network, but its members formed it as a way of networking with people who might provide members of their own organizations with publicity in return for information.

If you were in an extreme rush, you could try searching the Internet for the right person directly. For example, if you are the journalist looking for information about a piece of music and you are working late at night on the East Coast, you might search for the home page of a major West Coast university and look up members of the history department. If you found a professor whose posted biography indicates expertise in that area and includes an e-mail address, you could e-mail him, asking your question.

You are lucky because the message "becomes available to the recipient within seconds after it is sent—one reason why Internet mail has transformed the way that we are able to communicate,"[2] and the professor checks his e-mail just after his last class. Finding your query intriguing, he locates the information you want and sends it to you. You have what you need, and you got it from a network—but you were not really networking. The interchange has opened the door to networking with that professor in the future, but at the moment it lacks the mutuality implicit in real networking.

One way to enter this wired world is through your old networks. Ask people with whom you network if they use the Internet. When you find people who do, ask them whether they have joined discussion groups. Ask them which service provider they prefer—America Online, CompuServe, any of the dozens of others—and why? Ask which Web sites they visit most often. Why do they single those out? Where do they go for different categories of information?

In other words, do some research among those people you can usually depend on to have the kind of information you need. In the course of these discussions, you are likely to learn a great deal that will save you time and make your early attempts much more enjoyable. Moreover, the enthusiasm you will notice about this new way of connecting is likely to be extremely enticing; my own adventures into this world were prompted by hearing numerous discussions of intriguing information gathered by others on-line. Once you try it, you will never go back. However, you should be careful to avoid abandoning your old networks—those relationships remain invaluable, offering far more than information.

The Whys and Hows of Networking

Economist W. Brian Arthur points out that "for all its glitz and swagger, technology, and the whole interactive revved-up economy that goes with it, is merely an outer casing for our inner selves. And those inner selves, these primate souls of ours with their ancient social ways, change slowly. Or not at all."[3] While most of us come, albeit somewhat reluctantly, to accept the need to adapt to the changes taking place around us, the stress involved can be detrimental to our peace of mind or even our health.

Keeping this in mind, think about the best ways to relieve stress. For most of us, it involves understanding why we feel the way we do, and such understanding usually comes from sharing: we talk about our concerns both to relieve tension and to compare our reactions with those of others to make sure they fall into the range of what is considered normal. We all do this because we want to belong, to fit in: human beings are demonstrably social animals, with social ways. We seek human contact, we look for ways to connect with others, to build networks of individuals we can turn to when we need advice or help or information of a specific kind.

Principles of Traditional Networking

Building personal networks requires making connections with numerous individuals and then deciding if they are people you want in your network. You start by evaluating the contribution someone could make. For example, someone may be interesting, know a lot of people, and enjoy making introductions. Someone else may be a font of information—and enjoy sharing that information, sending clips of interesting articles about a subject you casually mention or that seems to them connected to you in some way.

As people are introduced into a network, members wait before evaluating the newcomers' value to the network. What is particularly pleasant about this traditional form is that if people do not add value, there is no pain in dropping them. No notification is necessary. They simply no longer receive calls. Those who prove responsive—for example, when asked about something, they work with other networks to get needed information and return calls in a reasonable time—become members in good standing.

Traditional networks are not mutually exclusive: they overlap in many ways. Because we think of this collection of networks in terms of the individuals to whom we are directly connected, we tend to forget that the individuals who make up our networks are connected to many networks that vastly extend our reach.

These kinds of networks are extremely flexible.[4] They tend to grow when we introduce someone to another participant in the network; in fact, in most cases, the full span of the network is not known to any of the participants. These networks occasionally involve face-to-face meetings between various—but far from all—members. They provide concrete value at various times to various members. And they continue to exist and add value only if members work to maintain them, responding to requests whenever possible, even reaching out to others to help them find solutions to problems. Active participation—the opposite of running into a meeting at the last moment to hand out business cards—is the key to building strong networks.

The ways in which members of networks communicate have evolved over time, with new forms of communications being added when they become commonplace. That raises the question, If networks that once required people to congregate in a given location changed to include written communication and ham radio and telephones that allow networking over long distances, why should the advent of electronic networks make a difference? The answer is simple. For established networks, there is probably little difference if, say, e-mail is added to the usual communications tools. But that's not the end of the story.

The New Networking

The advent of advanced information and communications technology has made a difference in the way new networks develop and the ways in which they work. Networks that have their start in the electronic world take a number of forms. Some of these networks are electronic "places" where people can go with the intent of forming or joining a group—and anyone with access to the technology and an understanding of the rules of the new game can gain entry.

Some are simply groups of people who want to keep informed about a specific subject, such as the many networks that have sprung up centering on providing members with information about a specific disease and serving as support groups for fellow sufferers. The networks we are focusing on in this chapter, however, are work relationships that are built around the electronic networks that have become the backbone of today's flexible organizations.

Not surprisingly, since the network of networks known as the Internet was built by people to improve their connectivity with people and organizations with whom they were already networking, there is an enormous similarity between the way electronic and personal networks are shaped. Once we can visualize how these networks are structured, they will seem far less complex. Remember, you do not need to know how to build them or the technologies underlying them—you need to know what they are and how to gain access to them. And you do need to know how to adapt to this new form of networking.

The Problems Inherent in Corporate Networking

As we saw in Chapter Four, the connectivity brought by electronic networks has created a number of changes in organizational structures and the ways in which business is done. Connected organizations are usually less hierarchical and more flexible in terms of workforce; in fact, John Huey, describing them in *Fortune* magazine, called them "fungible modules built around information networks, flexible work forces, outsourcing, and webs of strategic partnerships."[5] As a result, the old rules that guided our work lives have disappeared, and often the new ones are far from clear.

The failure of organizations to address the difficulties of networking to accomplish given tasks has led to an increase in uncertainty in many areas. When you work with people from different divisions or even different organizations, you often are not certain who will provide your performance review. You also wonder who is ultimately responsible and accountable for joint activities, and who is the ultimate stakeholder when it comes to a major project.

Many human resources and management issues involving networked work need to be resolved. For example, if a company has international teams, what has to be done to make sure that they work well together? The *Economist* points out that it is not the time differences that cause the problems, but "while the night shift in the average coal mine or paper plant lives just down the road from the day shift, the Tokyo bond-dealing team may never meet the chaps in New York, and analysts in Singapore may know their counterparts in London only through telephone conversations squeezed between the end of one day and the start of another."[6] Here, the lack of interaction caused by distance affects the building of corporate culture, with the attendant loyalty that a common culture brings.

Another example of a problem that emerges in the new workplace is the use of telecommuting. How does a manager who deals with a worker at home know if that person is coping well with the lack of personal involvement? At first managers feared that people would waste time, but the problem seems to be burnout instead— people feel they must spend endless hours at the computer to justify their working outside the office. The lack of personal connectivity between managers and employees is the problem here.

A far larger set of problems for business arises when electronic connections with other organizations are not thought of in strategic terms. For example, when the purchasing manager buys goods from another organization on-line, on the basis of cost or location and availability, building relationships with suppliers is often left out of the equation. But when managers who work on that basis need goods in short supply, they have no one to ask for the favor that will get them the goods when they need them. The failure to build relationships can be costly.

These issues are becoming the subject of a great deal of discussion in the business media and among human resources executives.

One way to avoid the uncertainty that causes so much anxiety is to raise questions. Ask where reports about team progress will be sent. Prepare a memo about your participation on teams, especially when the results have brought the organization concrete benefits, and bring it with you when you have your review. Ask whether those successes have been taken into consideration. When you work at home or manage someone who does, be certain that goals are set.

The other important part of working together on electronic networks is face time. Although in many situations involving long-term projects, relationship building can be done on-line, face-to-face meetings at some stage are important for negotiating complex arrangements. Indeed, "experience shows electronic communication to be most effective when it builds on face-to-face contact."[7] In other words, there are links to the old forms of networking that even the most sophisticated users of these new technologies are not comfortable abandoning. Herb Brody, an editor of *Technology Review*, notes that "Despite the Net's promise of creating a tightly connected, global community of researchers, several impediments block more widespread use. While collaboration through e-mail can work well once a professional relationship is established, there is not yet a good way to simply start chatting with someone without an introduction—the kind of thing that happens all the time when scientists rub elbows at a university or conference."[8] The personal element so key to traditional networking is also essential for managing the boundaries between organizations—especially when the relationships are electronic.

Rules for Electronic Networking

Underlying every relationship, no matter how personal, is a set of dynamic and negotiable understandings. The total absence of such understandings results in anarchy, and the uncertainty inherent in anarchy would keep corporations from the Internet. Their stakeholders would never put up with the amount of risk that anarchy implies; their reactions would be the same as if you suggested building a plant in a country that had a coup every year for the past seven years.

However, as Mitch Kapor, founder of Lotus (the company responsible for those enormously popular spreadsheets) says when discussing the Internet, "Inside every working anarchy, there's an old-boy network."[9] Indeed, "working anarchy" is a good definition of the Internet—anyone with the necessary equipment can connect at will and anyone who does not like what they encounter can decide not to use it. It works because it is, at heart, an old-boy network of people who work together to promote one another's interests—one of which is the continued growth of the Internet.

John Perry Barlow, who writes extensively on technological issues and is cofounder of the Electronic Frontier Foundation, an important organization involved in issues of freedom and responsibility in electronic communications, sums this up by saying that "in the absence of laws or any credible authority to impose them, human interaction [in cyberspace] has been ordered according to a more instinctive and pervasive sense of personal responsibility than most governments would impute to their citizenry."[10] In other words, the majority of users have concluded that without trust and adherence to a code, the whole system would collapse.

Not only does the system show no signs of collapse, all indications are that it is thriving. Moreover, the anarchy is well controlled. In interviewing dozens of young people who work with computers, I heard almost every one of them make these comments: "Information must be totally free. There are no rules and there shouldn't be," and, ironically, "You have to understand the rules." When I asked what the rules were, I received long lists of dos and don'ts, behaviors that were acceptable and those that were not. These rules often related to establishing trust in electronic relationships, an issue explored in the next chapter.

The comments about anarchy in the electronic world from people who hold more senior corporate positions focused on the need to protect corporate information, copyright and intellectual property rights, and information about personnel. When asked about rules, they discussed the rules governing passwords that had been put in place by their information technology groups before mentioning the rules governing e-mail etiquette, but they were emphatic about the need to have rules governing correspondence on-line, since it was so critical to the new networking.

Netiquette

Discussing the rules of electronic communication somehow makes the whole world of advanced information and communications technology seem simple. The rules govern behavior—writing clearly, being helpful, not wasting people's time, being a good on-line citizen. It seems more applicable to behavior at summer camp than in a scary place known as cyberspace. I think the plethora of rules that are out there say a lot about the culture of the Internet. Many of these rules are offered on-line; there are dozens of books devoted to the subject; there is a "Miss Manners" of e-mail; and one serious and useful book on the Internet devotes a full chapter to "The 100 Rules of Business Netiquette," explaining that there are separate sets of rules for Web sites, e-mail, and business principles.[11]

Of course, it is impossible to resist the lure of presenting one's own set of rules. My justification for presenting such a list for e-mail is that when you look at them and realize how very ordinary they are, it will make overcoming your fears about the on-line world a lot easier.

The Dos and Don'ts of E-Mail

- Keep your messages brief. Limit each message to one subject.
- Use correct English (jargon is a particular problem in e-mail), and be certain you check your spelling and grammar.
- Do not use all capitals to be emphatic—it is akin to screaming. Likewise, use those devices known as emoticons sparingly—and only when you know the recipient of your mail very well. (Emoticons are little pictures made by putting

together, say, a colon and a close parenthesis— :) —to indicate a smiling face. You can find whole lists of them by simply typing the word emoticon into any search engine's find-what box.)

- Make sure you describe your subject in a heading. In personal correspondence, also use your full name and address, and address the person to whom you are sending the message by his or her full name.

- Respond quickly. If you are going to be unavailable for more than a day, say so when you send a message.

- Keep in mind that what you say reflects on your organization if it is sent with your corporate address.

- Use bullet points to break up long messages.

- Watch what you say. Remember that any e-mail you send might be read by others, for example, if someone forwards your mail to someone else. This goes double for newsgroups, where anything you post may hang around in searchable archives for years.

- If you do not know the person to whom you are sending an e-mail message, explain how you got their address and why.

- No matter how flattened an organization you work for, do not send e-mail to someone who is a level above the person to whom you report to make a point or show how valuable you are.

- When replying to a message, unless you are replying right on the message itself, make certain you include enough information so the person knows which message you are responding to. "Yes" alone does not do the trick.

And from Virginia Shea's on-line book *Netiquette:*

- "Adhere to the same standards of behavior on-line that you follow in real life."[12]

These rules are all aimed at improving communication between people who are relating to one another, networking, electronically. As you will see in the next chapter, the last rule—
*Adhere to the same standards of behavior on-line that you follow in real
life*—is the key to trust.

Tips for Networking

Educate yourself about the basics of the new world of connectivity.

- Think about the ways electronic networks are similar to traditional networks and the ways they are different.
- Think about the advantages these networks provide in terms of reaching out to people and gaining access to information.
- Be aware of the negative aspects of new technology, such as the potential for invasion of privacy, and identify strategies for dealing with them.

Use your traditional network to help you adapt to the electronic network.

- Ask people in your network who are already on-line for practical help.
- Discuss your feelings about and compare your reaction to the changes you are experiencing with the people in your network.
- Supplement electronic communication with face-to-face communication.
- Keep your traditional network in place—you'll still need it.

Consider how connectivity affects your workplace.

- Pay attention to the ways electronic networks have changed organizational structures and procedures.
- Recognize that some degree of confusion is inevitable while new structures are still being developed. Raise questions about issues that are fuzzy.
- Get to know the networking rules your company establishes and think about their purposes, such as to protect proprietary information.

Learn both the codified and unwritten rules of netiquette.

- Think about how the rules of good behavior that apply to other human interaction can be adapted to this new arena.
- Look at some of the books and on-line lists of netiquette rules.

Chapter Seven

Learning to Trust in Electronic Relationships

Trust is, if anything, absolutely as important as the ozone layer for our survival.

—*Sissela Bok*[1]

Working in the new, flexible organizations that are becoming more and more the norm today involves building new relationships with people electronically. As discussed in Chapter Six, these relationships are a form of networking with employees who come and go as the company moves in different directions or with members of various divisions assigned to work together, often temporarily and without ever meeting. In addition, as organizations enter into alliances and outsourcing arrangements, employees have to deal with one another across organizational boundaries. Moreover, work today also involves handling information culled from various Web sites. The major issue in all these cases is trust, the fifth step in the framework.

Developing enough trust to work comfortably in rapidly changing situations poses problems because it is not always clear how our usual methods of determining who and what we trust should be adapted to meet the exigencies of these electronic relationships that develop in such different ways. Examining the similarities and differences between the way relationships were built traditionally and how they are built electronically can help clarify our thinking in this area and lead us to the answer to the question, How do advanced technologies affect our concepts of, belief in, and actions regarding trust, honesty, and ethics?

111

Is Trust Different in Cyberspace?

When it comes to the real, as opposed to the *virtual* (electronic) world, part of the discomfort so many feel is a result of their lack of knowledge of the beliefs about trust—or even of the existence of such beliefs—common to those who establish relationships online. How is trust different in this world? How is it the same? How do you decide who to trust and what sources of information to trust? And then there are issues that involve trust tangentially, such as security or privacy.

Starting Points

Tackling the problem of trust in the new world of technology begins with an analysis of established methods for building trust and determining how well they might apply in an on-line universe. Basically, trust is based on a perception of shared values and beliefs, a conviction that most people want to do things the right way. Many of us who are uncomfortable with the electronically connected world grew up assuming that the people we interacted with lived by the same version of the Golden Rule—"Do unto others . . ."—we did. We assumed that a sense of fairness, integrity, and honesty was the basis for the actions taken by other persons or by institutions; we assumed shared understanding as well as the goodwill and competence to carry out promises.

As we began to make connections with people and institutions that did not act in accordance with our cultural values, we began to think more about how to determine who and what to trust and to examine the ethical issues involved in much of what we encountered more deeply. But our world was somewhat limited. Today we not only lack the time to make considered judgments, we work in a globalized world where judgment is much more difficult than it was before everything became so heavily interconnected. The cultural differences that come into play may run counter to our assumptions about the rules people follow in business. The simplest example is pricing—haggling over prices is a norm in some cultures and is unexpected in others.

Trust in People

When it comes to the individuals in our personal and professional lives, traditionally we have built trust over time. We learned about someone's background as the relationship changed from chance encounters to friendship. We loaned a book, and it was returned; we decided to go someplace together, and our new acquaintance showed up when expected or called to explain why not; we attended a conference together and observed interactions with other people. We came to anticipate each other's behavior in different situations. We reached the point where we trusted each other.

Thus the first question to resolve when developing relationships on-line is, Can we make judgments as we always did? It is not an easy question to answer because we meet people on-line in many different ways. Listening to a discussion of chat groups between five men and women in their twenties who work for a high-tech company based in California, it became clear that those who have grown up with computers and the new connectivity take an approach that, at first hearing, seems wrong. I asked them how they make friends on-line and trust people they know nothing about. Their responses boiled down to this: "You trust people on-line until you learn they're not trustworthy—or until you think about meeting them, then you have to start asking the hard questions."

When you think about it, it is quite a logical answer. There is no reason to attribute all the baggage that comes with meeting strangers in other settings to meeting strangers on-line—you are not in their physical environment. People who are heavily involved in computers often join chat groups on the Internet using fake names and frequently describe themselves in ways that bear little resemblance to reality. These encounters tend to be a form of entertainment. They can move these chats into another kind of relationship, say, by agreeing to send e-mail back and forth and then carefully arranging meetings in public places.

Professional Relationships On-Line

While half of all jobs in the 1950s involved the generation, processing, retrieval, or distribution of information, some estimate that by the turn of the century, 95 percent of jobs will involve working with information. Some experts add that "most of this information handling will involve computers and advanced communications devices."[2]

When it comes to working in this environment, we often find ourselves on teams with people we have never met who work in different divisions, whose abilities we don't know, and whose objectives aren't clear. Or we find ourselves working with a counterpart in another company to manage a business relationship set up by senior management to gain a strategic advantage. How do we know whether we can trust that person?

For example, say you work for a small company that has decided to outsource its marketing function. The person who hired you and was training you leaves for a new job, seeking growth opportunities lost as a result of the outsourcing arrangement. The vice president to whom your boss reported asks you to manage the relationship with the marketing organization until a decision is made about replacing your boss.

Delighted by this opportunity, you call the marketing organization and discover that your company's account is being handled by someone in an office in another city. You contact that person and the two of you try to figure out how to work together. You receive little guidance from your vice president, except a reminder to keep your eye on deadlines and expenses. When you ask about the specifics of the work to be handled by the marketers, you're told that the contract is for $100,000 over the next two years and that the vice president will "look for documentation" in the files your former boss turned over to him.

Your contact says that she has a copy of the marketing strategy that was agreed upon and will fax it to you immediately, then asks where you want to start. This is someone you have never met, with whom you now have to make decisions, and make them in light of arrangements you had no part in. Trust? Who do you trust? The vice president who has not been very helpful? The contact at the marketing company? Her agenda is a total mystery to you.

Making this work may be the opportunity of a lifetime. Your company is known for giving people a chance for advancement—that's why you accepted a job there in the first place. Then you think about the woman you'll be working with. What kind of pressure could she be under to save her company as much money as possible by doing as little for you as she can? Or is this her opportunity to create a magnificent campaign and develop her own reputation?

So you begin to do a little checking. You call a friend whose father is in marketing and ask her to get you any information she can. You talk to people who belong to the same branch of the American Marketing Association as you do. In other words, you network. In the process, you find out a lot, and none of what you learn seems frightening. Time to take a deep breath and decide to give this a try.

Over the next couple of months, however, even as the two of you begin to make the projects you are handling work, you remain uncomfortable. Phone calls and e-mail can take you only so far. So one day the two of you decide to meet for lunch at a halfway point—about a hundred miles from each of you. After talking about life in general and sharing career stories, you decide this is not only someone you can work with—she is someone you like.

Then, during the course of the year, as problems develop and are solved, trust grows between the two of you. The trust between you did not spring up out of thin air. In was built on a bed of information, knowledge carefully collected, and was cemented by experience. In other words, it was not all that different from building trust before computers.

The Corporation and Trust

When it comes to organizations, trust involves reputation—which of course is built on the behavior of the people who work for those organizations. According to management expert W. Edwards Deming, unless there is trust "there can be no cooperation between people, teams, departments, divisions. Without trust, each component will protect its own immediate interests to its own long-term detriment, and to the detriment of the entire system."[3]

Corporate cooperation in the future will be between companies as well as between divisions of a single company. Suppliers will need to get into customers' databases to check inventories; marketing groups hired to handle a part of a publicity campaign will need to tap into the corporate database for mailing lists; temporary workers will be on-line in all areas of the business. The judicious combination of an environment that fosters integrity, the awareness of a need for adequate security, and a clear interest in protecting privacy are needed to make all this work.

Leadership Action

Ensuring a culture in which trust can flourish in these situations is the job of the organization's leaders. Leaders must keep in mind that their behavior sets the example for everyone in the organization. Those leaders who are most effective at transmitting their values and beliefs are not embarrassed to speak out on what many call soft or "New Age" beliefs.

Among the actions leaders can take to instill a culture of trust is to put in place a credo that publicly proclaims the organization's ethics and then demand that senior management live up to those standards. Companies should also put codes of ethics in place and appoint ethics officers. Establishing ongoing education and training programs aimed at reinforcing those codes and including ethics as part of performance reviews may also help. The issue of electronic security—the need to protect the company by not giving out passwords or allowing others access to company computers—must be part of the training. Leaders must make it very clear that part of their companies' standards involves protecting clients and customers from those who would harm them by accessing information found on-line.

Can You Trust Their Security?

When it comes to business transactions on-line, lack of trust is clearly a major obstacle. In fact, a recent *Business Week* Harris Poll reports that 61 percent of respondents "would be more likely to start using the Internet" if the privacy of their "personal information and communications would be protected." People worry about the kind of information that can be obtained from computers. Here we are dealing with a lack of trust in the ability of companies to maintain security and protect privacy, but it may be an extension of the general erosion of our belief in people's trustworthiness: in 1993, only 39 percent of Americans believed that "most people" can be trusted, a fall from 58 percent in 1960.[4]

When it comes to using computers for financial transactions, the numbers are even worse: *Business Week* reported that 80 percent of all respondents in the survey said that they were somewhat or very concerned about the security of their personal financial information when "buying a product on-line by credit card"—or giving their "credit card number to a catalog phone service representative."[5] The last point is important, because compared to Internet sales, which were $500 million in 1996 and are projected by Forrester Research to reach $7 billion in 2000, catalog revenues are $50 billion a year.[6]

Clearly, part of the problem is that people just don't have the familiarity with buying on-line that they do with catalog purchasing. They may not really feel comfortable giving out credit card numbers to catalog phone representatives, but they have enough experience (their own and that accumulated through stories by friends and the media) of doing so that they can ignore that uneasiness.

Trust in on-line buying is likely to improve in the future for two reasons. First, advances are constantly being made in the area of security. Companies designed to help other companies put fire walls and encryption devices in place to prevent theft of information are proliferating. In fact, given that the fastest-growing electronic businesses involve stocks and the sale of goods, the lack of media focus on this issue is an indication of how little it is a problem. Credit card fraud in this nation has reached about $500 million a year, but the amount of such fraud on-line is considered "statistically insignificant."

The other reason such purchases will become more common is that we will gain experience with them and come to recognize that the same precautions used to avoid such problems with catalog companies can be effective here. When deciding whether or not to place an order, if you recognize the name of the company and know it is considered reputable, you go ahead; if you don't, you may check with friends or the Better Business Bureau. The same rules can work here.

You have to take responsibility for protecting yourself on-line because many companies have simply not yet begun to devote adequate attention to the problem. A survey by the American Management Association revealed that security procedures are woefully lacking at most companies, although "more than one out of every six respondent Fortune 1000 corporations said they had already experienced negative effects associated with inappropriate Internet usage involving their employees, and at least one of ten have already been involved in a legal claim related to an employee's use of information technology."[7]

This failure to put such policies in place is not a result of great trust that nothing will happen—it is a result of systematic corporate inattention to a new issue because it has not yet affected the bottom line or damaged reputations. Security will become more and more important the more companies encounter problems and the more they turn to electronic commerce as a way of doing business. When deciding who to trust on-line is important, the experience companies have in these areas and the industry they are in both make a difference. Banks are far ahead simply because security has always been a critical success factor for them; in the same way, Amazon.com, a pioneer in on-line sales, has focused on security issues because it discovered that ameliorating such concerns was critical to its ability to lure customers into buying on-line.

What Do "They" Know About You?

For many people, the anxiety about this new technology centers on the kinds of information that can be assembled about them as a result of the widespread use of computers. If our medical records are on-line, are they secure? Is anyone able to find out how we spend our time, what we buy, who we associate with, how much money we have?

Computers provide those who want information about us for personal or business reasons the means to assemble huge amounts of it. When you sign the release of information authorization on your insurance form in order to get reimbursed for medical expenses, when you provide a bank or loan company with your sources of income, when you make a credit card purchase, you are providing data.

Before the age of computers, companies putting this information together found it an extremely time-consuming and costly process. Today, it is so efficient that if you wanted to hide information such as a chronic condition when you are thinking of switching jobs, you would find it very hard to do. For example, even if you do not ask for reimbursement from your insurance company for a prescription because that could result in a potential employer's learning about your condition, just filling the prescription and paying out of your own pocket can give you away. The information about your purchase of the prescription is recorded in a number of databanks.

Another set of problems created by this pervasive information collecting results from inaccuracy. Professor Richard O. Mason of Southern Methodist University says that what we need to worry about here is: "Who is responsible for the authenticity, fidelity and accuracy of information? Similarly, who is to be held accountable for errors in information and how is the injured party to be made whole?"[8]

Overcoming your anxiety about these issues requires knowing what actions are possible so that you can take a role in supporting or fighting various rules and regulations. The ethical questions involved in the collection and use of on-line information are far from resolved. This is an area where you must keep up with developments, learn what you can about the issues, take part in public discussions—in other words, make sure your voice is heard.

For example, the Federal Trade Commission is looking into the use of privacy notices by companies who engage in on-line business and is threatening to impose regulations if companies don't begin to adopt such policies. Alan Westin of Columbia University, who publishes the *Privacy and American Business* newsletter, says that companies are going to have to begin to post and adhere to the policies put forth in such notices not only to prevent government regulation but to ensure that electronic commerce on the Internet keeps growing and that advertising on it flourishes.[9]

Another aspect of security involves guarding company secrets such as proprietary information, and avoiding improper use by employees. A survey by Gordon & Glickson, a major law firm with both Washington and Chicago offices, found that "more than one out of four respondent Fortune 1000 corporations do not have formal policies regarding company trade secrets, and almost three out of five do not have policies regarding Internet usage."

In addition to policies addressing all these issues, however, companies—even those who do not do business on-line—are going to have to put in place and constantly improve their electronic safe-guards. It is the only way they can ensure the security of proprietary information.

What Can Technology Tell Your Boss About You?

Two issues bother people most when it comes to their privacy in a workplace dominated by advanced computer technology: constant scrutiny and the ownership of e-mail.

Computerized work involves built-in supervision. Computers record what we are doing and how long we spend doing it. Employ-ers are delighted because it helps eliminate the need for supervisory personnel. In fact, today, there are computers set up to distribute work to employees. They also calculate how much time each task sent to a computer should take to complete by averaging past per-formances by a range of employees. Once the work is assigned, it has to be completed in a given time; there is no one to take into account that you came to work with a terrible headache or cold. How do you explain that to a machine?

If you work for a company that expects you to answer to a machine, you are working for a company that does not exhibit much of the quality we are discussing here—trust. That company will eventually pay a price for its behavior. For example, when unemployment falls, as it has in the last few years of the 1990s, companies such as this are the ones that will experience the effects of low morale, constant employee turnover, bad word of mouth, and perhaps worst of all, a lack of innovation and creativity.

The issues surrounding e-mail privacy also are the subject of much discussion. Employees worry about others' reading their e-mail, especially their supervisors. What is interesting here is the assumption that an employee is free to use the company's equip-ment to write personal letters that might embarrass the company or someone in it—and to do so on the company's time. The answer to the question of e-mail privacy is simple—you should assume that the company may look at your e-mail. If you want to communicate privately by e-mail, you will simply have to get a home computer and use it for that purpose.

Trust in Information

Another place where the issue of trust arises because of the Internet is in the realm of information. The abundance of information available on the Internet is startling. Enthusiasts tell you that everything you'll ever need to know is on-line—and free. Moreover, they add, the search engines available—Yahoo!, AltaVista, Lycos, Magellan, Excite, Infoseek—make it possible to find information any time you want it. Unlike a library, the Internet never closes down.

But keep in mind that when you use the Internet to access information, it is great fun, but not simple—and not necessarily reliable. Depending on which search engine you choose, you get a different number of matches (places where the word appears), sometimes broken down into different categories such as newspapers or chat groups, sometimes listed in a single mass. Furthermore, depending on what you want the information for, you have to put some effort into determining whether the information you find is worth having.

A few numbers from a recent article in *Science* magazine will make the problem clear: there are approximately 320 million indexable pages on the World Wide Web. The engines that search the Web for information will often come up with quite different information because the "indexing patterns of the engines vary significantly over time." Moreover, documents may no longer exist or have been changed, and pages are indexed only if they are registered with a given search engine. None of the individual search engines covers more than 35 percent of the indexable Web, but "combining the results of the six [major] engines yields about 3.5 times as many documents on average as compared with the results from only one engine."[10]

To check the value of this new tool for yourself, ask someone you know who is "connected" to give you an hour to help you look up something—say, the *Titanic*. When the two of you are sitting in front of the computer, your friend will place the cursor on various icons on the screen, click the mouse to connect to the Internet, and then call up a search engine. If you were doing this in early May 1998 and used the search engine AltaVista and asked it for information on the *Titanic*, in less than a minute the screen would have indicated that there were 395,600 matches.

That seems like a ridiculous number, but, according to most estimates, the number of documents available on-line grows by 10,000 a day. Of course, you can refine your search; you can, for example, tell the search engine to require that a match contain both the word *Titanic* and the name Leonardo DiCaprio, and now you would discover that only 18 percent of the 395,600 matches contain both.

Your friend will call up some of the documents that contain the matches; some will be entertaining, some will be informative, some will seem pointless, some could even be offensive. Suddenly the stories of people spending endless hours on-line make sense. You asked for an hour, but you keep wanting to see a little more. Most people admit that during the first weeks they were on-line they behaved like addicts, losing track of time.

The main problem is not so much narrowing down your searches as determining what information you can trust to be fair and accurate. After all, anyone is free to post whatever they want on-line. Even when articles are posted on university sites, there is no way to determine their validity. They may be posted by students as well as professors. They may contain material plagiarized from others. Because they appear alongside documents from magazines and reputable sources does not mean anything. There are no screening committees to decide who may or may not post material on the Internet.

Drawing Your Line in the Sand

You know what to trust when searching for information the old-fashioned way: you have a lifetime of experience in assessing sources that began with your first trip to the school library. You trust an article that appears in, say, *Science* magazine because somewhere along the line you learned that any article that appears in that magazine has been reviewed by experts in the area before being accepted for publication. When you pick up a newspaper, you know to what degree you can trust the information it contains. When discussing current events, you will be comfortable citing the *New York Times,* want to check the facts before citing the *New York Post,* and never dream of citing the *National Enquirer.* For academics, the same is true of books; a Harvard University Press book is greeted quite differently from one published by a vanity press, where authors pay to have their books published. Some small percentage of those books may be solid and well researched, but others may be on such offbeat topics or might be so poorly written that no mainstream publisher would take them. Overall, because they are not subject to prepublication review of any kind, they are not generally reliable.

The variety of material that appears on the Internet raises additional questions. An undergraduate at a major university recently turned in a paper in which some rather questionable facts were attributed to a "working paper" by someone at another name university. When questioned by his professor, the student explained that he had found the paper on the Internet. The professor called a colleague at the other university to ask about the author of the paper. The colleague checked and discovered that the writer was an undergraduate—and the paper had received a low grade.

The point of this is not that you should stay away, stick to the library, and shun electronic information. Instead, you need to figure out how to deal with this abundance, a way to find the clues or signals that will help you through the plethora of information.

The first step is to be a critical reader. Ask yourself if what you are reading makes sense in light of what you already know. Ask yourself a series of questions: Who is the author? What is the author's affiliation? What else has the author written? Hard questions? Not if you are on-line. All you need to do is search some more. Look for references to other materials by that person. Who published that material? Now check the person's affiliation. Look for other articles on the subject and check the footnotes. What are the standard sources in that field? Try locating experts through chat groups dedicated to the area you are exploring and ask members for good sources of information.

Information Safety

Many groups already are at work trying to put in place gatekeepers and standards when it comes to information, a move that angers the ardent advocates of this new technological universe who believe it should be totally free of all restraints. Gatekeepers and standards are, however, a logical solution to the problems that have developed as the electronic world has opened up to include so many of us.

This point has particular relevance to the worlds of medicine, science, and technology. More than a hundred peer-reviewed journals in these fields were on-line at the end of 1995. By the end of 1996, that increased substantially; one publisher alone, Elsevier, is planning to have eleven hundred such journals available electronically to subscribing institutions in the near future. But this is just the tip of the iceberg.

Because of the increasing costs of journals in print and the slow process of peer review that limits the speed with which articles appear even in the peer-reviewed on-line journals, there are now many *preprint forums*, where articles are released to the academic community while still essentially in process.[11] The greatest difficulty is that this provisional material becomes available to a general audience that does not understand the need for further review and checking before accepting the conclusions.

Trust in Society

In the new world that technology is creating, power, authority, and wealth will accrue to those who can use these tools. Since the growing inequality of wealth and income in this nation has been a cause for alarm, resulting as it does in an unhappy citizenry that distrusts those who govern, it may be in our self-interest to ensure that everyone has access.

However, we must accept the ramifications of making such a decision. Someone will have to pay for it. If government is to take on this responsibility, it will mean higher taxes for a while. If in the end, however, it improves economic growth because people acquire some sophistication in the use of technology, thus becoming more employable, the screaming will die down, and it will be proclaimed a worthwhile expense. If business is asked to assume some of the responsibility because it will need workers with these skills in the future, what will it demand in return in the short term? Are we talking only about teaching people how to use new technology? Or are we also going to have to find ways to provide those who can't afford it with the equipment they need? Can we do it through public libraries? And will those who are dependent on publicly provided tools for access be afraid to use it because they fear it will be used to collect information about them? It all gets back to trust.

A Good Beginning

There are many groups who are engaged in the issues of ethics and trust in the electronic world. One of the things many of these groups do is codify rules for computer use and users. One of the most common documents in this area is the Ten Commandments of Computer Ethics. The version presented here was developed by the Computer Ethics Institute of Washington, D.C.[12]

The Ten Commandments of Computer Ethics

1. Thou shalt not use a computer to harm other people.

2. Thou shalt not interfere with other people's computer work.

3. Thou shalt not snoop around in other people's computer files.

4. Thou shalt not use a computer to steal.

5. Thou shalt not use a computer to bear false witness.

6. Thou shalt not copy or use proprietary software for which you have not paid.

7. Thou shalt not use other people's computer resources without authorization or proper compensation.

8. Thou shalt not appropriate other people's intellectual output.

9. Thou shalt think about the social consequences of the program you are writing or the system you are designing [or the work you are doing].

10. Thou shalt always use a computer in ways that ensure consideration and respect for your fellow humans.

As a first step in building electronic relationships, you might send the commandments to people you meet electronically, casually saying something about finding them interesting. Then open a discussion about the topic. Whether the person you are discussing the commandments with agrees that they have merit—or disagrees with some specific points (or even laughs about the whole thing)—you will learn something about what your contact believes and is likely to do. It can help in your efforts to determine how much you want to trust someone you have never met.

Conclusion

As you begin to enter this new world, keep in mind that trust is not built overnight. It is the result of experience. Before this new age dawned, we all met people and companies who disappointed us by their actions. Again, remember that just because you are dealing with someone through technology does not mean that all your experiences are irrelevant. You are just as likely to encounter disappointments in the electronic world as you were before—and you are just as likely to encounter integrity, loyalty, and honesty. The faces in both worlds are human, which is very reassuring since your future success in the world of work is dependent on your ability to overcome your anxieties about these new technologies.

At this point, you should be more comfortable with change, understand the new world of work, and have some confidence in your ability to notice changes on the horizon. In addition, you have an idea of how the new connectivity works and how to begin to trust in this new world. Now it is time to think about something far more concrete—what skills you need and how to acquire them. You are ready to take the next step—to become someone who fits in the new world of work.

Tips for Coping: Trust

When building relationships on-line, you should take the same care as you do when meeting new people in other ways.

- Get to know people by interacting with them over time.
- Learn the differences between the culture of older methods of communications and the culture of the Internet.
- When you meet someone face to face for the first time, choose your meeting place with care.
- Ask members of your networks for information about companies and people you work with on-line.
- Allow trust to grow naturally based on the knowledge and experience you acquire as the relationship progresses.

Remember that you can use the same skills you developed as a smart consumer in the electronic marketplace.

- Check out the reputations of the companies you deal with.
- Don't give out information to representatives of companies you don't know.
- Remain alert to the loss of privacy that results from the proliferation of electronic databases.
- Advocate with corporations and government agencies for the establishment of tight security systems and high ethical standards.
- Report Internet fraud to appropriate government agencies.

Since there are no gatekeepers on the Internet, you must establish your own criteria for judging the worth of what you find on-line.

- Be vigilant about establishing the authenticity of information you find on-line.
- Use your knowledge and experience to identify possible errors.
- Validate postings by finding out about the author and scrutinizing the author's sources.
- Check out the reliability of Web sites, but remember that even the sites of peer-reviewed journals may post works-in-progress that have not been vetted.

Chapter Eight

The Art of Reinvention

I got most of my business experience in a world
which no longer exists. If I were to tell you how
I got ahead in that world, it wouldn't do you any
good. If you want to know how to drive a modern
car, you don't go to someone who can tell you, out
of the richness of his experience, the tried and true
principles by which he once succeeded in
chauffeuring a horse and buggy.

—*Edward A. Filene, 1936*[1]

Filene's words are just as applicable today as they were more than
sixty years ago. The changes in organizational form that have
resulted in flatter, less hierarchical structures eliminated layers of
middle management, bringing to an end a major career path that
was the norm from the post–World War II economic boom to the
late 1980s, and placing new demands on all workers. Every worker
today needs, in addition to skills for specific tasks, skills that were
once the province of middle managers: workers must be able to
communicate, innovate, train, lead, negotiate.

In addition, the change from manufacturing to services—and
particularly to what is called knowledge work—has changed the
nature of the skill sets workers need. Moreover, the advances in
information and communications technology have made technology into one of the largest and still-growing industries, creating
hundreds of thousands of jobs involving work that did not exist
thirty years ago. Finally, technological advances also have changed

the skills people need to do older kinds of work, changed our relationships to work, and often changed where we do our work. And the changes are still coming.

With the advent of knowledge work, according to Don Tapscott in *The Digital Economy*, "an organization will be competitive only if it can learn faster than either its current or emerging competitors. Any firm can have the same technology as another company; any product can be copied."[2] He goes on to point out that the only competitive edge a company can count on will come from "lifelong organizational learning."

The changes that have taken place in organizations have affected not only the way organizations operate, but the way employees must think about their futures in those organizations. You need to learn new skills because the organization for which you work is adopting new ways to handle old processes and embarking on businesses that follow different models.

The question is, How can you succeed in a world where, as Filene noted, the only experience you have is in a world that no longer exists? How can you reinvent yourself so you can become part of your new world? To begin, of course, you need to understand something about the new ways business is being done so you can determine how your skills fit, and then you have to decide the kind of work you want to be involved with in the future so you can invest in reinventing yourself for that kind of work.

This chapter explores the need to reinvent yourself as an employee or entrepreneur so that you fit the new world of business. It is the sixth step in the framework, but not the last, for as soon as you find a way to fit in the new world of work, you must begin to look around for the next wave of changes to be certain you have a head start on success when that wave sweeps through the workforce.

New Processes, New Ways

Three changes made possible by advances in information and communications technology—business process reengineering (BPR), electronic data interchange (EDI), and team structures—have dramatically altered many of the old ways work was done. At the same time, these advances created a whole new world of business—electronic commerce—and a new industrial sector—technology. A basic understanding of each of these will make clear some of the new paths to success in the new world of work. Once again, understanding what is happening is the first step in coping with the demands of this new world of work in an age of connectivity.

The Costs and Benefits of BPR

BPR is a technique used to break down the activities involved in important processes and determine the value of each step. By asking what is being done and why, it is possible to isolate those activities and tasks "that don't add value or are redundant and, consequently, are candidates for BPR—that is, candidates for rethinking and redesign. For example, in many companies, the same set of activities, under different names, may be performed by different groups in the company or at different locations. . . . The two locations may have different procedures and different systems for handling these activities, which may in fact be able to be addressed by a common system, which would enable the company to save money because it could get bulk discounts and the operation can be handled by fewer people."[3]

BPR has not always proved successful, however. In fact, Michael Hammer, whose article "Reengineering Work: Don't Automate, Obliterate," published in *Harvard Business Review* in the summer of 1990, brought BPR to the world, was among the first to admit that unless an organization made BPR a part of a whole corporate makeover it would fail most of the time. As a result of the failures, the techniques used to redesign the business processes were refined and integrated with advances in technology to change the way businesses did work, which made these efforts far more successful. At the same time, those companies with problems found that the downsizings that resulted from reengineering their organizations provided an easy solution to immediate problems with their bottom lines. Wall Street was quick to reward even the announcement of layoffs, to the relief of many CEOs with companies that were floundering.

Case Study.   Even when the goal was purely efficiency, smaller workforces were the usual result of BPR. The following, from personal observation,[4] is a good example of how BPR along with the introduction of new technology can change an organization. For more than 160 years, Friends Provident, an insurance and investment company in the United Kingdom, maintained a reputation for taking good care of customers. In the early 1990s, the company managed assets of almost £14 billion (U.S. $22.4 billion) for two-and-a-half million individual policyholders and tens of thousands of members in groups. In 1993, it paid benefits of £990 million to policyholders.

Friends, like most other insurance and investment companies, was for a very long time a "paper factory," with numerous agents generating sales in dozens of branch offices around the country that resulted in policies that had to be sent back and forth to main offices for approvals and contracts—and then for billing and collection. In the 1970s, the company turned to technology to improve service, lower costs, and improve efficiency and accuracy. The result was a traditional, mainframe-based information technology system.

That system served well through the 1980s, enabling the company to keep up with the legislative and administrative changes that were affecting all players in the British insurance industry. But in the early 1990s, it suddenly faced an oversupplied insurance market that led to increased competition resulting in some market consolidations; in fact, it was involved in two mergers. The shakeout that was taking place in the industry made acquiring new business and lowering costs imperative.

In 1992, the company decided the time had come for a thorough reexamination of the technology being used to serve customers so as to revamp business processes. The first step was a workflow management study. Taking into account the company's size—4,000 employees, 4 administration centers, 70 branch offices, 3.5 million customers; its systems—traditional IBM mainframe with dumb terminals; and the need to change, it undertook a thorough process review.

The analysis of the processes in place revealed that, for example, more than 40 percent of the time of those involved in customer service was spent on pure paper pushing, not on the insurance business. For example, it took thirty-seven different steps to alter an existing policy, which although a typical transaction, was nevertheless a fairly complex activity that would greatly benefit from automation. The initial reaction was skeptical. It became far less so when the analysts were able to show that a major part of those steps were a result of the fact that any given piece of paper flowing through the system came to rest numerous times to allow those dealing with it to locate additional information or obtain approvals for the changes requested. These suspensions of activity could not be eliminated until all the information about a policy was available at the push of a button.

What was needed was a new information technology system that would work with the systems already in place to change the information from a potential policyholder's application as it was received on a form to a readable screen on a terminal; the information on that screen would serve as the initial record to which new information would be added. Moreover, the information would be accessible to everyone who had to handle the policy at any time on an as-needed basis. The new system would eliminate photocopying, filing and refiling, numerous printouts, and transmissions of documents to and from various locations, thus reducing unproductive overhead. Furthermore, the new technology would manage business process procedures as well as staff resources, for example, letting each clerk know what to do to make the targets for any given work period. And, equally important, the new system would support changes driven by the users.

Friends bought a system from DST Systems of Kansas City that could address workflow management. The system not only moved policies and associated information through the organization with great ease, it dramatically reduced the "float time" of paper moving from one location to another because it could transmit the electronic customer file to any employee in any other location across the country who had the needed expertise to address specific customer requirements.

In addition, the system allowed the company to move work from a location experiencing an overflow to a location that had a temporary shortage of work—all the locations could function as a single work area. The implications for companies that operate in multiple time zones are enormous in terms of reducing overtime costs.

The company reduced the total size of the workforce as a result (although a number of new technologists were hired to maintain the system and help solve problems with it as they emerged), saving millions while continuing to provide good customer service. In addition, many managers retired or found other work because they could see that the assignment of work by machine had made their positions redundant. The company did, however, invest heavily in training its original customer sales representatives to use the new technology.

EDI and the Supply Chain

Another change in processes was the result of the development of EDI, which let companies transfer business documents from computer to computer securely even when various systems in different divisions or business units were incompatible. EDI simplifies the exchange of routine business transactions and allows the integration of information throughout all the divisions of a business, eliminating numerous steps in the process of getting goods out the door. In other words, it eliminates paperwork by redesigning the flow of paper through the supply chain—the series of steps that begins with the order and delivery of raw materials to a manufacturer that makes a product and then packages, stores, and finally sells and ships it to retailers who in turn get it into the hands of consumers. Each step requires transportation of materials and often warehousing. And each step requires orders and invoices and bills of lading and so forth, which must be generated and sent from party to party.

The supply chain just described, however, is the physical supply chain. Improving the processes involved in moving and manufacturing and shipping brings some benefits. Reducing the flow of paper that is involved in all those steps—say, by making it possible for orders to be placed and paid for electronically—brings additional benefits. Indeed, when companies realized the savings from these steps, they began to assess their whole supply chains to see if they could use EDI to improve them in other ways.

Companies such as Benetton that analyzed their processes as part of the BPR that preceded adoption of EDI found that they were duplicating steps along the way, that warehousing could be cut by producing products just in time, and that distribution centers could be consolidated. It did not take long for the results of these improvements in both the physical and information flow to have a major effect on the bottom line. In a 1996 study of the pharmaceutical industry, A.T. Kearney, Inc., reported that pharmaceutical companies that were leaders in supply chain management had an 18 percent higher return on earnings than other companies surveyed.

EDI and supply chain improvement eliminated many back office jobs, reducing the numbers of distribution centers and increasing the use of alternate shipping arrangements, often eliminating trucking fleets. It required hiring employees to deal with the specific technologies, finding the right people to manage the relationships with suppliers and customers, and making changes in marketing and sales. Today, companies are finding that the Internet can be used to do all the things companies once turned to EDI to do—more efficiently and at far less cost. Useful as it is, however, the switch to the Internet as the backbone of the supply chain is likely to cause further disruptions in the workforce.

Teams

The 1980s brought to prominence the value of teams as a means of improving performance, particularly in manufacturing. U.S. automobile manufacturers were suffering from the invasion of Japanese imports, which were increasingly capturing market share because of their high quality. American companies rushed to adopt Total Quality Management (TQM), the tool introduced to the Japanese by W. Edwards Deming, an American who went to Japan with his ideas when they were rejected at home.

At the heart of TQM was the concept of quality teams, and by the 1990s the idea of teams had taken hold in the United States. In 1993, the publication of *The Wisdom of Teams: Creating the High-Performance Organization*, an examination of the value of teams by Jon R. Katzenbach and Douglas K. Smith of McKinsey & Company, brought the theory into common practice. Hundreds of thousands of workers found themselves part of teams, with somewhat mixed results.

The early successes achieved by Motorola and 3M, followed by a turnaround in the automobile industry after the introduction of TQM there, made teams a part of the workplace. Today, people are expected to know how to work in a team and sometimes are even hired on the basis of how well they perform in tests that involve team interaction. The skills needed for team work—and for managing teams—have become a necessity in some organizations. However, because both management and team members are often unskilled in areas needed for building successful teams, problems occur that make these attempts less valuable. These problems become worse when teams are composed of individuals who do not work in the same physical location or belong to the same company. The trouble is often the result of a lack of clear communication between project sponsors and the team and between team members themselves, and it heats up when there are rival political agendas that do not get resolved.

Electronic Commerce

One of the hot new areas of business growth is electronic commerce, which includes both on-line sales from businesses to consumers and business-to-business transactions.[5] It also involves the marketing of products and services on-line to build brand recognition and the exchange of information to facilitate research and development or speed and simplify the processes involved in buying and selling, managing inventory, billing, delivery, and so forth (an extended version of the supply chain).

The most commonly cited figures about electronic commerce, from Volpe, Welty & Co. of San Francisco, show that 95,000 companies worldwide were involved in electronic commerce in 1995; that number grew to 135,000 in 1997 and is expected to reach 435,000 by 2000. As for revenues, projections by Forrester Research of Cambridge, Massachusetts, show that companies engaged in business-to-business uses of the Internet will gain $66 billion in revenues by 2000, financial services companies will generate $23 billion, and those selling to consumers will realize $7 billion. The projected growth is startling: "Businesses will exchange an estimated $17 billion in goods and services this year over the Net. By 2002, that's expected to top $327 billion, says Forrester Research Inc."[6]

One of the most startling developments is the number of businesses that have sprung up and exist only on the Web, such as Amazon.com, the world's largest—and first—on-line bookstore. These new enterprises have thrown established companies in their industries into the roles of fast followers. Barnes & Noble, the largest bookstore chain in the United States, decided to move into electronic commerce in response to the emergence of what it saw as a new form of competition. Although Barnesandnoble.com has a long way to go to match Amazon.com's $400 million in sales in 1997, it did earn $14 million the same year—its first year of operation.

Leonard Riggio, the head of Barnes & Noble, made a strategic decision to set up a separate business unit to compete in this area after a thorough strategic analysis that convinced him that on-line sales will not seriously cut into his stores' profit margins. He has done this as a first step to what he sees as a whole new world of publishing, one in which bookstores are places where "customers could tap into millions of titles and print any part from these works on the spot." He looks ahead to "software programs that could point customers to specific lines in various books, threaded by a single topic, or ones that could ferret out and print obscure texts that never made it into book form. . . . The change in the next ten years will be much more profound than what has happened in the last ten."[7]

Case Study. Other businesses have made conscious decisions to move simultaneously into intrabusiness, business-to-consumer, business-to-business, and even consumer-to-business electronic commerce. One that has done so successfully is a thirty-five-year-old Dallas-based employee placement firm specializing in financial services, accounting and administration, legal, engineering, information technology, and IT consulting with fifty-five locations in the United States and Canada.[8]

The company's entry into electronic commerce began in 1995 when a new vice president of marketing suggested that the firm use its existing IT infrastructure to develop a presence on the Internet. This infrastructure had been developed over the preceding few years to maintain the firm's national database of some one million résumés (the largest in the staffing industry) and facilitate communication among the various offices and headquarters.

The move into electronic commerce seemed particularly appropriate given the company's involvement with applicants who had expertise in IT and financial services, groups that tend to be especially Net savvy. Moreover, the expertise needed to fill positions in the IT arena, especially for projects involving the Year 2000 computer problem, might just be available in other areas of the world.

The new VP's goal was to create a Web site and use the Internet not only as a new channel, but also as a new marketing medium. He convinced management to let him run a pilot project for a new Web site that, among other things, posted job openings. A year later, Web-generated revenues were $1.2 million. Some 2,000 to 2,500 people entered the site each day and looked at an average of 4.5 pages. These "hits" generate 200 to 250 leads per day and result in about one placement for every 1,000 leads.

The company, pleased with these early results, decided to make electronic commerce a larger part of its strategy. It hired the technical expertise needed to enlarge and maintain the site, and it also broadened the content to include an annual salary survey and career-path information that would draw people back to the site. But the highlight of the site remains the listing of job openings that includes descriptions of available positions and the job requirements.

The company also has integrated its e-commerce activities into its total marketing strategy. It does cross-medium advertising by attaching its Web address to print advertisements, journal ads, and promotional material. It also advertises on high-traffic sites such as Netscape to draw attention to its site.

These examples highlight the fact that electronic commerce is going to be bringing enormous changes in work in the future. The skills that will be needed by these companies often are very different from those their current employees have; marketing on the Internet is different from traditional marketing and designing a Web page requires special skills. What kinds of jobs will be eliminated by the developments of the future—such as Riggio's new forms of publishing? What kinds of technological jobs will be of most value? The workforce for electronic commerce is not yet known, but clearly watching developments and becoming as comfortable with these new technologies as possible is a step in the right direction, especially if you are in an industry such as used car sales or stock brokerage that is already experiencing on-line competition.

From Silicon Alley to Silicon Valley

According to the American Electronics Association, the number of technology-related businesses reached 152,203 in 1997; high-tech companies exported $171 billion worth of goods, twice the amount exported in 1990; and the technology industry added 200,000 jobs between 1996 and 1997, bringing its total number of workers to 4.5 million. Technology companies make up some 13 percent of the Standard & Poor's 500. The average wage of a technology worker in California in 1997 was $57,971—and California has more lower-paid assembly and staff workers than areas such as Washington State, where the average wage was $66,752.[9]

Those numbers don't seem overwhelming by themselves, but think about the number of people involved in information technology in other sectors. For example, colleges and universities, marketing firms, hospitals, hotels, grocery chains, and so forth all have large staffs of technologists. While these workers do not necessarily earn as much as those who create the applications and design the hardware for the major technology firms, they tend to be fairly well paid.

Technology companies are models of the new flattened organizations. Andrew Grove, founder of Intel, works in an open cubicle that is very like those used by the company's programmers and analysts. These organizations feature the kind of teamwork and exchange of ideas that are conducive to the innovation and new developments typical of the knowledge enterprise. These firms also tend to cluster together geographically (for example, in the region around San Jose, California—near Stanford University—known as Silicon Valley, in Manhattan's Silicon Alley, and in clusters near Silver Spring, Maryland, and Cambridge, Massachusetts), which means that employees know one another and frequently hear about projects that intrigue them, which leads them to move around frequently. The result is a lot of cross-fertilization, as people interested in learning more and being part of the latest technology share ideas, some joining together to start new enterprises.

The growth of the Internet and new technologies surrounding it are likely to affect this sector even more, spurring additional growth and creating new kinds of jobs. Entrepreneurs in this area are finding that venture capitalists are eager to reach deep into their well-lined pockets to finance start-ups, particularly in the area of multimedia. Much of this kind of work is done on-line, from home. These companies are taking the word *virtual* to new levels.

The Skills Upheaval

Now that we have a somewhat clearer picture of the changes that companies have made in their processes as well as in their organizational form, some of the ways in which job requirements have changed are clearer. As you read what follows, keep in mind what you learned from Chapter Four about the nature of the employment you want—in terms of both how far toward the information age you can move comfortably and where you are in your life and work cycle.

The failures firms experienced when first working with BPR and with team structures were the result of their failure to examine their organizations holistically and integrate them strategically before moving ahead. If you can begin to think of work as it relates to your goals at any given point and the kind of situation in which you are most likely to thrive as well as the skills needed, you will have a far easier time adding the missing pieces—specific sets of skills.

From this examination of the ways in which organizations reinvented the way work is done, five broad categories of job changes emerge: jobs that produce the same outcome but are done using some new tools; jobs that are migrating to a new environment that requires changes in thinking as well as in tools; alterations in the meaning of management as well as how managing gets done; jobs that did not exist before; and portable skills in search of an occupation.

Tools That Automate Part of a Job

Remember the real estate assessor mentioned in Chapter Four, who works with a handheld electronic device? He is now a part of the world of technology because of the little device he uses to transmit the information he collects. Countless companies have turned to sophisticated systems that coordinate the information provided by a worker with a simple-to-learn device that accepts information and returns instructions. The complex systems behind these handheld devices are often of little or no interest to the employee, who is trained for a day or two in the device's operation.

The trucking industry has turned to this model, using computer systems to provide information about pickups and deliveries, timing, cost, mileage, and routes to those who sell the shipping services. The ability to provide accurate estimates of cost and on-time delivery as a result of the information collected through the devices used by the truckers helps these salespeople build strong customer relationships. For the salespeople, there is more technology to learn, but it has been built to be as easy for them to use as possible. For the trucker, "it still all boils down to a human being loading, unloading, and driving a truck."[10]

Changes such as these take place all the time in the world of work. Some simple changes introduced one at a time can eventually create a fairly savvy technologist. A number of people working as mail room clerks in a leading insurance company in the Midwest were taught how to check incoming documents by scanning bar codes, to run documents through more sophisticated scanning devices in accordance with the directions implied by those codes, and to instruct the machine where to send them. They eventually began to find ways to overcome jams and other problems with the machines. They were also responsible for photocopying, for the postage machines, and for using computers to confirm deliveries with Federal Express electronically.

Over time, these workers accumulated a great deal of knowledge. When the personnel department noticed that mail room staff were leaving after about two years—and going to technology companies—the company decided to offer them opportunities for advanced training with its own information technology department and many moved up the career ladder into the real world of technology. Approaching technology one step at a time makes learning easy and comfortable; eventually you accumulate a body of knowledge that will stand you in good stead when further changes occur.

New Thinking and New Tools

At the same time that so many jobs are being lost as a result of changes brought by information technology (remember those insurance agents who are being replaced by customer service representatives with screens full of information?), according to Ward Hanson of Stanford University some 100,000 people may already have found jobs on the Internet as "cybermediaries." Many sales representatives who once sold the old-fashioned way, by appearing in the offices of those who needed their product and hoping for a little face time, are now selling a rapidly increasing percentage of their goods on-line to corporate purchasing departments.[11]

This mix of the old and new is also the key to growth in fields such as marketing. Here you are not merely adding new technological tools, but must also rethink the customer and the medium and the strategic implications of what you are doing. When adding the electronically connected world to your usual world, adaptation requires aligning a totally new approach with the old. You have to learn to ask a new set of questions in order to plan a campaign that takes both worlds into account.

The New Meanings of Managing

"In the authoritarian organization, managing is the responsibility of managers. . . . Thinking is separated from doing, power is disconnected from accountability, control is imposed on people from without rather than from within, and measurement supports evaluation not improvement."[12] More than a quarter of a million middle managers lost their jobs as the authoritarian behemoths of the old order flattened and downsized in the late 1980s and early 1990s. These were the people who had expertise and skills in a number of areas because they had usually worked their way up the organization, but were more involved in oversight than in actual, measurable tasks. They conveyed the orders from the top to the workers who had to carry them out and communicated back up the chain of command, analyzing performance, calculating profits and losses for their groups, and writing reports that explained what was happening in their departments. They were also responsible for seeing to it that new employees understood the organization's goals and, at times, they were the people who trained their subordinates in the skills specific to their function.

Today, the people who still hold managerial titles have a very different set of responsibilities. First, they are expected to maintain skills in an area of expertise so they can serve as the leaders of work groups and provide hands-on management of tasks. Second, they are supposed to be able to be so involved with the projects they are managing that they can instruct and mentor the people they are working with and stimulate rather than inhibit creativity.

Today's managers must know the right way to praise ideas, promote innovation, foster creativity, reward initiative, and encourage risk taking. They must incorporate people working at home or in other companies, temporary workers, and part-time workers into their thinking. They must use new technological tools to review and react to suggestions from employees quickly so people don't feel that making suggestions is a waste of time. They must also react carefully so employees are willing to put ideas forth without the fear that they will be told that a proposal is stupid or worthless, which takes learning to write criticisms that will be read in solitude where words can be misinterpreted.

New managers must provide employees with time to experiment and learn. Brainstorming sessions that do not have to have a clear deliverable, freedom to acquire tools and books, an opportunity to work on a concept—these are all part of encouraging the kind of environment in which creativity flourishes. This again is particularly difficult when much of the activity goes on where it isn't visible.

Another major change that has taken place is the spread of leadership down the organization. In examining the workforce today, one rapidly discovers that there has been a significant increase in people who are not managers or supervisors who "have direct supervisory responsibilities."[13] Clearly, the need for supervision and management has not disappeared, but rather has been spread out among workers at other levels. Companies running lean—keeping the permanent workforce small with the idea of adding workers to respond to market demand as needed—assume that when extra workers are brought in, whether on a contingent, part-time, temporary, contract, or even full-time basis, their full-time, core employees will take on more and more management and supervisory responsibilities. When the company is running tight, all its employees have to have specific skills that make them valuable. In other words, you must maintain up-to-date specific, task-oriented skills— and also have the skills in communications, human relations, analysis, and strategy that were always the province of managers.

New Jobs from New Processes

In early 1998, the Information Technology Association of America reported that there were about 190,000 jobs in the information technology area that were unfilled—about half in the information industry.[14]

The changes in the supply chain and the development of electronic commerce have opened up two new job categories, which both take understanding the new technologies but require quite different sets of skills: negotiation and boundary management. Many of the people assigned to teams to help rework processes have ended up losing their old jobs (say, as warehouse managers as five warehouses became two because of just-in-time manufacturing), but discovered that handling the negotiations between the sales forces of various divisions over the flow of goods created a position that did not exist before. Those on these teams can often show the need for the new position and have a strong argument for being given a chance to fill it.

When companies undertake large projects, "boundary managers are responsible for resolving conflicts between different organizations, different sponsors, and different groups of management, and all without distracting the members of the team. There are times when boundary management involves dealing with differences of purpose and values. Boundary management requires an intuitive ability to raise issues that are about to create problems and resolve them before they become major impediments to progress."[15] Van Campbell, vice chairman of Dow Corning, explains that "you not only have to deal with the business, you also constantly have to deal with the relationship you have with the partner—nurturing it and maintaining high-level contacts, so that when you deal with items of substance you will be dealing with friends, people you understand and respect."[16]

Another set of new jobs comes out of the new on-line enterprises and technology companies. More than half of American businesses employ fewer than one hundred people, the fastest-growing segment is entrepreneurship; 42 percent of business activity takes place in non-stock-traded businesses. If you can acquire the skills, these companies may provide you with the opportunity to achieve the American dream; they are the traditional road to success for many workers. In the area of technology, the stock options given the first employees to join Bill Gates at Microsoft or Larry Ellison at Oracle have created an astonishing number of millionaires. (Because these people are so devoted to the continued advance of technology, and because they enjoy their work enormously, it is not unusual to discover that a programmer working sixteen hours a day in a Silicon Valley cubicle is one of those millionaires.)

When it comes to the newest of these enterprises, the ones growing up around the Internet, the possibilities are unbounded. The phenomenal growth rate indicates that there is likely to be a continuing strong need for people with Internet-related skills; in the few short years since the Internet reached public consciousness, the number of people working for Net-related companies went from a handful to some 760,000 in 1997.[17]

Transferable Skills and Lost Arts

The next category of change as a result of technological advances includes the category that is most anxiety-provoking—the elimination of categories of skilled work. Remember the printer and the nurse we met in Chapter Two. The only answer for the printer was to examine his experiences and knowledge, discover what portable skills he had built up, and find a new way to use them. The case of the nurse is somewhat different—she has in essence switched careers, moving from nurse to knowledge worker, applying her expertise to the building of technologies that will help make hospitals more efficient and economical.

The lessons they learned as they moved on are, however, a valuable part of the learning we all must do as we continue to reinvent ourselves to match the needs of the organizations that employ us.

What Tools Do We Need and How Do We Get Them?

When asked about the thirty thousand students a year that are dropping out of school to jump into the booming technology job market, James L. Beug, chairman of computer sciences at Caltech, says, "My fear is that these kids will last about seven years on the job market. If they haven't learned to learn and can't go sideways into management, what happens to them?"[18] His words highlight the areas we have to focus on as we move forward: learning to learn, especially specific technology skills, and learning the skills once associated with management—communication and leadership.

One step will be to abandon the overwhelming anger and anxiety so many of us feel because of the actions of corporations during the makeover of businesses that took place during the late 1980s and early 1990s and still hasn't ended. The changes that took place were necessary. The discomfort was the price we paid for our currently booming economy. Those of us who want to move ahead in this environment instead of just holding on can find hope in some of today's actions of these corporations. They have come to realize that they must play a role in ensuring that they have the workers they need with the skills they need to survive in a knowledge economy.

For example, Motorola has embarked on a massive transformation program. As part of that program, "Human skills required to make the company prosper are all being reinvented. New learning skills are being instilled through huge investment in learning research. Company education programs and learning skills are being exported into the community and the local school system in an effort to retrain tomorrow's employees, customers, and suppliers."[19]

The government has also recognized the need to provide opportunities for learning. In January 1998, the Clinton administration announced that the government would embark upon new initiatives aimed at training programmers. The administration targeted $28 million dollars to this effort. As part of the plan, the "Labor Department will offer $3 million in grants to schools, businesses and local governments to retrain laid-off workers as programmers." In a related effort, "The Commerce Department will spend $17 billion to bring technology resources, including training, to poor people."[20]

These actions make it clear that corporations and the government have begun to accept the need to help employees constantly replenish their skill sets. As individuals, we have to find ways to take advantage of this new awareness. We can start by developing our capacity to learn at the same time as we are learning both new general skills and specific skills. It is a tall order, but the path is clear: to succeed you must accept that adapting to the new world of work created by the advent of advanced technologies requires, at the very least, enhancing the skills you already have, and that success in the new world of work probably requires finding new kinds of work to do as well as acquiring the skills to do it.

Tips for Coping: Reinvention

Take a careful look at the new ways business will be done in the future.

- Find out how new business processes and new industrial sectors are likely to change your work life.
- Think about what jobs are likely to be eliminated, and research new job opportunities that are likely to develop.
- Pay attention to the changes that are taking place in the division of labor.
- Be on the lookout for new job descriptions that are being invented to meet new needs.
- Decide where you personally can fit in best and are most likely to thrive.

Prepare yourself for your job of the future.

- Take an inventory of the skills you already have, and decide what new skills you will need to acquire.
- Prepare yourself for the new style of leadership with skills in such areas as training, communications, and human relations.
- Be sure to consider those skills—such as negotiating—that are becoming more and more important in keeping the new processes running smoothly.

Seek out opportunities to learn the skills you will need to add to your skill set.

- Look for ways to build on your skills and knowledge in your area of expertise so you stay up-to-date.
- Take advantage of opportunities at work to become involved in the change process, and use the process itself both to identify future opportunities and to build new skills.
- Keep abreast of technological changes and decide what technical skills you need to meet your goals.
- Make learning about technology easier and using it more comfortable by taking it one step at a time.

Use the process of learning specific skills and knowledge to enhance your ability to learn to learn.

Chapter Nine

Looking Beyond Tomorrow

> No one needs to be reminded that times are
> changing, whatever disagreement there may be as
> to the character of the change which is taking
> place. To the majority, probably, the change has no
> discernible character. They do not see *a* change,
> but many changes, and the changes which they do
> observe do not seem to have any particular relation
> to each other.
>
> —*Edward A. Filene*[1]

The changes that are taking place today are related to one another
even though, much like the development of steam power, electricity, and railroads—the impetus to the industrial revolution—they
may look on the surface as if they are separate changes. Businesses
have changed not just because of global competition but also
because of the new technology (which helped bring about globalization), and so has health care. The world of finance has changed
and so has agriculture. The multitude of new inventions that com-
bine to make possible the advances in information and communications technology that have enabled those changes and countless
others mark only the beginning of the age of information.

Forecasters looking to the future tend to limit their predictions
to changes they see as a result of further changes in the technologies that are now available. The twists are endless, ranging from
sensor technologies that will allow us to share an embrace with a
lover in another nation or allow a doctor to operate robotically on

a patient three thousand miles away to artificial intelligence that will make it possible for advanced computers to make decisions of every possible sort and run our businesses and control our lives.

Forecasters do not try to predict the move to yet another age because we have only entered this new age. The scope of changes that may still come seems so vast that looking even further seems impossible. Moreover, when you put together various trends that can have an impact on one another, you get pictures of startling changes that are more than enough fodder for the imagination. For example, many are beginning to express deep concern about the fact that in the industrial countries, birthrates are falling below replacement rates. While this is not yet true in third world countries, rates there also have begun to decline. According to United Nations population data, since 1965 "the fertility rate in the third world has been cut in half"—down from six children to three per woman.[2] There is much speculation that technology has produced this result through the changes it has made in lifestyles (working women, uncertainty). If that is true, what will happen if those same changes occur in the less developed nations? Will the developments now taking place in the technologies of cloning be our answer if everybody is too busy working to have children? Or, to reach out further in our speculations, will we turn to space travel to look for other worlds to trade with to keep our economy strong? What would a connected universe mean? In other words, looking ahead to speculate on an age of space exploration or human reengineering still sounds like science fiction when we have so far to go in the age we have just entered.

The Seven Questions

From the outset, the purpose of the book was to try to answer seven questions about the changes that advances in information and communications technology have brought and are likely to bring in the near future:

- What is the nature of the new technologies?
- What changes will they continue to bring?

- How will these technologies affect our concepts of, belief in, and actions when it comes to trust, honesty, and ethics?
- How will the changes brought by these technologies affect our relationships with others?
- What impact will these changes have on business and how will that affect us on a personal level?
- What do we need to do to cope with these changes?
- What will happen to those who are left behind, disenfranchised from the future by lack of access to technology or appropriate education?

The answers to these questions come out of the discussions of the steps to the framework in the last six chapters; here they are presented in capsule form as a reminder that the changes wrought by the new technologies have only begun and that their ultimate impact is not yet clear. We are partway down such a circuitous path that we cannot see where it is leading us.

- *What is the nature of the new technologies?*

The new technologies really offer two things: a way to help manipulate data to produce information that can be used to build knowledge, and a way of communicating that information. In more detail, the new information age is based on machines—computers—that apply arithmetical processes to data that is fed into them in digital form. The end result of that process is the transformation of data into information that can be accessed in many different forms and that can be combined with other information to produce even more information.

The addition of means of communicating the information in any machine to any other machines via wires, fiber-optic cables, or the air (using satellites) allows the growth of information as each machine that is able to communicate shares its information with all the other machines with which it communicates. As the number of computers sharing this information grows, so does the knowledge that can be culled from the information.

The total amount of information available in this network of connected computers sounds overwhelming, but every individual computer can be used to access as much information as the user wants or needs. In fact, most users access a mere fraction of the information available, using software to provide the machine with instructions on what to do with specific information. Even when individuals have access to the network of networks of computers known as the Internet, the amount of information accessed is limited by the time, needs, capabilities, and desires of its users.

The new technologies thus allow individuals and organizations to capture, store, manipulate, access, share, and communicate information. Depending on the knowledge and intent of their users, these machines can be used to write letters that will be sent via the Postal Service if the user decides to print the letter, put it in an envelope, put a stamp on it, and take it to a mailbox—or via e-mail if the user elects to push a few keys or click on a mouse. These computers can be used to send a friend a recipe or to work with a team to design an airplane. They can be used to buy and sell goods, and they can be used to provide information that can prevent a disaster or cause one. The uses to which these machines are put are the responsibility of the human beings who own and operate them: the nature of these machines is, at least for the foreseeable future, a reflection of human nature.

- *What changes will they continue to bring?*

The changes that advances in technology have already brought have altered almost every aspect of human life. They have affected our personal lives: some geographically dispersed families have become far closer as photos are scanned and sent, as information about important milestones is shared, and as immediate concerns are resolved in a group setting—and all quickly and relatively inexpensively. At the same time, our friends may be people we have never met in person who share our interests, drawing us away from old friendships developed as a result of physical proximity.

Another set of changes has to do with the idea of community. As more and more of us go on-line, we are in danger of losing the sense of local community that leads to civic responsibility. If schooling is done on-line, where would our schoolmates reside? If friendship has no connection with location, why join clubs or centers? If we shop on-line, what community benefits? Who should worry about libraries for those too poor to be on-line?

To date, the spread of these new technologies into our everyday lives has not been pervasive enough to make these questions critical. In fact, the only area where they have had major effects is, as we shall see in more detail in a subsequent question, in the world of work. In that world, categories of employment have disappeared and numerous others are in imminent danger of disappearing. The scope of the changes is an uncanny reminder of the switch from the agricultural to industrial age, which displaced so many in the workforce. Painful as this is for many, there is another side: new categories of employment have appeared at a rapid rate. For example, today, more Americans are employed in the manufacture of computers than of cars.

There is yet another aspect of these changes that must be taken into consideration. Although change has brought a great deal of pain and disruption to individuals, overall the economy has improved, just as it did in the last great shift: "In 1800 about 85 percent of the British population lived at or near the poverty line, where most of the people had always lived. A century later, less than a third of the British population was in poverty."[3]

- *How will these technologies affect our concepts of, belief in, and actions when it comes to trust, honesty, and ethics?*

Our concepts and beliefs when it comes to trust, honesty, and ethics are not affected by these new technologies, although we may have to change the way we act to ensure that our beliefs are shared. For example, we can apply our values and our understanding to the relationships we develop on-line. We can insist that those we deal with on-line, whether as friends, colleagues, or sources or purchasers of goods, adhere to similar values by refusing to connect to them if they do not.

The future may change this answer depending on the other changes that take place as a result of this new technology. Remember the quote at the beginning of the chapter? How do other changes relate to this change? What if the new technologies become so all-consuming to our youth that they spend less and less time connected to family at ever earlier ages? How can we instill in them our beliefs and concepts if they are part of a world of people we don't know, peers we have never met? We can't. Our ethics should move us to ensure that we maintain enough involvement in our children's lives that we pass along our beliefs. Not to do so would be to violate them.

When it comes to information, we must develop new criteria for establishing trust, guidelines that will help us weigh and measure what we find when we search for knowledge. For example, many people go on-line to find medical information. While there are numerous support groups for those afflicted by various diseases that provide solid and sensible information, the amount of misinformation that is circulating on-line, especially about so-called breakthroughs, has created a great deal of concern. As a result, established, well-known medical organizations such as the *Journal of the American Medical Association*, the *New England Journal of Medicine*, and the National Library of Medicine have set up sites that can provide sound information as well as links to other reputable sites.

The other issues in this area are privacy and security, particularly the battles over encryption. Here, each of us, whether we are on-line now or not, is responsible for keeping up with developments, particularly government initiatives, and making our voices heard in the debates between those who believe there is no need to impose controls of any sort and those who advocate restrictions that may in the end reduce the value and scope of these networks that now are so essential to so many aspects of our society and our lives.

- *How will the changes brought by these technologies affect our relationships with others?*

In terms of personal relationships, there should be only small effects. Again, it is in the world of business that the effects are dramatic. For one thing, we cannot avoid relationships in that world, and relationships that do not involve one-on-one contact require handling in very different ways: we need to network more to gain information to give us the comfort of knowledge. After all, these relationships must be built without the usual signals we use to judge character.

Moreover, the kinds of connections that are being made between organizations involve a totally new set of relationships that often make it difficult for the people who have to relate to one another. We need to think about many complex issues in order to develop the appropriate relationships. In other words, we need to ask ourselves such questions as, Who are the stakeholders in these relationships? How do we really understand the politics involved? How can we judge what is really critical? Managing these complex corporate relationships and relating to the people with whom we have to deal on a more personal day-to-day, but still distant, basis will take a great deal of ingenuity and learning. It is one of the major challenges of the new connectivity, and it is closely tied to trust.

- *What impact will these changes have on business and how will that affect us on a personal level?*

As we have seen, these advanced technologies have changed the very structure of organizations and the nature of work. Organizations have become far less hierarchical (and paternal), reducing the need for middle management and spreading the tasks once associated with middle management throughout the organization, requiring workers to learn new skills. They have turned to teams to improve quality, again demanding that workers have new and different skills, often cross-training team members to enable them to do multiple tasks. Organizations also have become more flexible, changing the nature of the work that they do in response to market demands and becoming lean enough in their core organizations to make it through periods of change, but able to gear up by adding contingent, temporary, and part-time workers when needed. They also outsource those areas that they do not consider their core competencies, which has provided work for displaced and entrepreneurial workers once attached to large corporations. (The problem is that workers usually do not do as well financially under these arrangements, although some enjoy the way of life.)

And the changes are far from over. As Philip B. Evans and Thomas S. Wurster point out in an article in the *Harvard Business Review*, "The changing economics of information threaten to undermine established value chains in many sectors of the economy, requiring virtually every company to rethink its strategy—not incrementally, but fundamentally. What will happen, for instance, to category killers such as Toys "R" Us and Home Depot when a search engine on the Internet gives consumers more choice than any store? What will be the point of having a supplier relationship with General Electric when it posts its purchasing requirements on an Internet bulletin board and entertains bids from anybody inclined to respond? What will happen to health care providers and insurers if a uniform electronic format for patient records eliminates a major barrier that today discourages patients from switching hospitals and doctors?"[4] Evans and Wurster are pointing to the whole burgeoning field of electronic commerce, which is likely to bring enormous additional changes to the world of work. In addition, there is a whole new area opening up: the field of technology—work both in technology companies and with technology departments in companies that do other things.

All these changes in our business organizations have already changed the nature of work: more work is knowledge work than physical labor, job stability is tenuous at best, there is more demand for creativity, people are expected to control their own time, where one works is changing, rewards are less certain, and there is more opportunity to choose the kind of future one wants. The last has an enormous downside because of the uncertainty—and usually lower wages at least in the beginning—involved in careers that are amalgams of different associations with employers. Here the kinds of skills one can acquire are key: "When a new technology comes in, usually the better-educated workers are better at adapting to the technology," says Kevin Murphy, economist at the University of Chicago. "But," he adds, "eventually, everyone learns and the premium for knowledge falls back."[5]

In other words, to stay ahead, you must constantly be acquiring new knowledge and skills.

- *What do we need to do to cope with these changes?*

The way to stay ahead, to succeed, is to keep abreast of change and learn skills that will ensure your employability—and then start learning the next set. Since most people find it hardest to gear up to learn and change when they are facing uncertainty, we must begin to accept the idea of learning to learn and then engage in a lifetime of continual learning.

Estimates are that a technical degree today provides skills that last about five years. In fact, "although many of the critical skills required in the high performance workplace have not changed (e.g., science, engineering, finance, and law), the pace of knowledge advancement requires constant updating. . . . According to the American Society for Training and Development, by the year 2000, 75 percent of the current workforce will need to be retrained just to keep up."[6]

- *What will happen to those who are left behind, disenfranchised from the future by lack of access to technology or appropriate education?*

These new technologies offer enormous opportunities, but as yet the opportunities are not available on an equal basis. Doris Graber of the University of Illinois at Chicago says that the "Internet revolution is largely a revolution of the currently or soon-to-be affluent well-educated males. . . . Eighty-five percent of all U.S. and Canadian users are white, while the source population is only 73 percent Caucasian. . . . Twenty-five percent of the Internet user population earns over $80,000 annually, compared to only 10 percent of the population in general. The median income, depressed by the sizeable number of students on the Web, is $40,000."[7]

Compounding the problem is the fact that the changes these technologies have brought to the world of work have increased the gap in income and wealth. A study commissioned by the National Planning Association's Committee on the New American Realities found that "the restructuring of organizations and jobs appears to be directly responsible for at least some of the changes in the wage structure. Recent job displacements, for example, have shifted more people to the lower end of the income distribution."[8] Attempts to address this issue are under way. For example, by 1996 there were over a thousand nonprofit Internet service providers who were operating with the aid of funds raised in the private sector and government grants; these groups were serving about 600,000 Americans.[9] However, when it comes to schools, there is a direct correlation between the affluence of a school district and the number of computers it has.

As a nation we are going to have to find ways to ensure that everybody has access or risk the danger of the kind of increasing split between upper and lower classes that foments unrest. More important, we must not forget those in the rest of the world. At the moment there are pockets of technology, such as Bangalore in India (home to some of the computer programmers who keep Silicon Valley in inexpensive code), that are moving to first-world standards of living. Yet these programmers who do so well by Indian standards are paid far less than equivalent American workers, taking work from Americans and not spreading wealth throughout the nation. The result is an increasing divide between the haves and have-nots in both nations.

With the rapid spread of information made possible through these new technologies, these inequities cannot remain a secret; at that point, redress will be critical. We owe it to ourselves to ensure that the world is a better place for all. Literacy, education, health, all the societal goods should be treated as the common heritage of humankind. Connectivity will not be forgiving when it comes to this issue.

There Is Joy on the Other Side

The problems of access and equity and the pain and dislocation brought by the changes that have already taken place are one side of the coin. There is no escaping the fact that many workers are so disillusioned about the world of work that the retirement age across the industrialized nations has been dropping steadily through the 1990s. Human beings just do not, for the most part, deal well with change. And do not make the mistake of thinking that it is just those who are afraid of technology who are fearful. The following exchange, from a roundtable discussion of the future of computing and telecommunications, shows how pervasive uncertainty is.

In the course of the discussion, the dean of the School of Computer Science at Carnegie Mellon University, when asked if he thought the pace of innovation would slow down, said he believed that "we have absolutely no control over the pace of innovation. It will happen whether we like it or not."

The senior research scientist at the MIT Laboratory for Computer Science replied, "I wasn't suggesting that we had any control over its pace, but you're saying you think it will continue to be just as fast and chaotic?" The dean responded: "And most of us will be left behind, actually."

At that point, the corporate vice president of applied research at Bellcore (the former executive director of the Communications Sciences Research Division at Bell Labs), chimed in, "At Bell Labs, we used to talk about research in terms of 10 years. Now you can hardly see two weeks ahead in our field. . . . the future is coming at us so fast that I sometimes find myself looking in the rear-view mirror."[10]

For all that these changes at times seem overwhelming, they can also be exhilarating. It depends on your mind-set. Tom Brown, who has written more than three hundred articles for major magazines and has been a commentator on National Public Radio, is one of the people who understands the new connectivity and has thought long and hard about its significance. He has developed the noncommercial "MG" Web site (*http://www.managementgeneral. com*), which presents new ideas from leading thinkers on community, organizational, and personal leadership. He is also the author of what are truly the first electronic books.

Recently, the *New York Times* presented an article on what it— and the manufacturers—called electronic books. Basically, the story was about new devices for reading printed books. Tom Brown instead rethought the concept of a "book." He writes his books on-line and offers them free for the Internet reader. The books are divided into *chaplets*, small chunks that appear in a narrower-than-full-screen format so as to be easy to read on-line. Each chaplet includes original art presented in color, notably e-paintings by cyberartist Mac Thornton. Because of the readability of typefaces chosen, you do not have the instant impulse to print the pages, although they can be printed easily. The reader is invited to comment on each new chaplet, and the comments are taken into account in his constant revisions—thus, each new reader gets the most current version of the book.

Brown reports that the number of readers who access the site has expanded wildly: since the Web site was started in February 1997, the number of readers scanning its pages has jumped from a handful to almost 16,000 hits per week during the summer of 1998 to almost 40,000 per week in February 1999. Formal reviews of his e-books have already started to appear, but perhaps the most important development is that Jerry Pepper of the University of Minnesota–Duluth decided to use Brown's innovative *Anatomy of Fire* as the only required text in an experimental course on group leadership that was completely paperless.

Pepper explained that he experimented with a new course structure and approach "after students requested that the Internet become more prominent in [the school's] academic regimen." Based on student response, he has already decided to use the book, its artwork, and other parts of Brown's Web site in his full-semester classes, starting in fall 1998. "Almost every aspect of the course that traditionally would be in paper form—from the syllabus to discussion handouts and, eventually, even examinations—will be online," Pepper said. Not surprisingly, both Brown and Pepper have been approached by other university professors with similar interests for their own courses.

Tom Brown calls this "electronic leveraging": as more and more people spread the word electronically, his Web pages and e-books are moving into the classroom and print media. It is a multimedia world we live in and therein lies much of the excitement about—and the reason for becoming a part of—connectivity.

Three chapters of this book have begun with quotations from Edward A. Filene, a philanthropist of the 1920s and 1930s who truly believed that business and social progress go hand in hand and that change is good. One of his legacies was The Century Foundation (founded in 1919 and known as the Twentieth Century Fund until July 1998), with which I have been associated for more than twenty-five years. The foundation's bylaws call for it to engage in research about critical social, economic, and political issues and to disseminate the results of its findings in accessible form to citizens, policymakers, and the media.

For some seven decades, the findings of studies sponsored by the foundation were released to the public only in printed form. Today, the organization has a Web site (www.tcf.org); it has also set up a second Web site devoted to the issues surrounding Social Security and its future (www.socsec.org), and it sets up on-line forums and discussions about critical issues. It also continues to publish important books and reports—and to post material from those publications on its Web site.

Everyone involved in the foundation has had to adapt to the changes brought by technology; in part, because of the heritage of

Filene's thinking, we have not only adapted to the new world of connectivity, we have embraced it. It is only fitting that this book close with the same words with which it began, Filene's words:

> The simple fact is that we have come into a new world, and the charts of the world we used to live in no longer serve our needs. A new human society is being born. There are no new laws; but the law of Nature is the law of change, and new times necessitating a new attitude.

Notes

Preface

1. Edward A. Filene, *Successful Living in This Machine Age* (New York: Simon & Schuster, 1932), p. 4. Filene was a successful retailer (Filene's department stores), a liberal, and a philanthropist who believed that business and social advancement go hand in hand. He founded The Century Foundation, originally named the Twentieth Century Fund, in 1919.
2. Nicholas Negroponte, *Being Digital* (New York: Knopf, 1995), p. 7.
3. Ferdinand Mount, "No End in Sight," *Times Literary Supplement*, May 3, 1996, p. 30.

Chapter One

1. Gene Koretz, "Which Way Are Wages Headed?" *Business Week*, September 21, 1998, p. 26.
2. Flemming Larsen, "The United States as a Job Creation Machine: An Example for Germany?" *Economic Perspectives*, USIA Electronic Journal, 3(1), February 1998. Available at *http://usiahq.usis.usemb.se/journals/ites/0298/ijee/larsen.htm* as of April 16, 1999.
3. Larsen, "The United States as a Job Creation Machine," p. 7.
4. Nicholas Wade, "Method and Madness: Future Non-Shock," *New York Times Sunday Magazine*, January 16, 1994, p. 14.
5. Basic information about the history of change management techniques is explored in Beverly Goldberg and John G. Sifonis,

167

Dynamic Planning: The Art of Managing Beyond Tomorrow (New York: Oxford University Press, 1994), pp. 219–235 and associated notes.

Chapter Two

1. This interview took place in 1996; the interviewee, who is still with the hospital, reviewed the material presented here and requested a few changes in wording as well as some changes in the personal information presented in the interest of privacy. These changes, which in no way affect the main points of the story, were made. In dozens of other interviews for this and similar consulting projects, such stories of displacement were common.
2. From Chapter Six of *The Prince*, which Niccolo Machiavelli wrote in 1513.
3. Edward A. Filene, *Speaking of Change: A Selection of Speeches and Articles* (Kingsport, Tenn.: Kingsport Press, 1939), pp. 224–225.
4. *The Wall Street Journal Almanac, 1998* (New York: Ballantine, 1998), p. 242.
5. Richard Saul Wurman, *Information Anxiety* (New York: Bantam Books, 1989), p. 32.
6. Stephen H. Wildstrom, "A Computer User's Manifesto," *Business Week*, September 28, 1998, p. 18.
7. Richard W. Riley, "Connecting Classrooms, Computers, and Communities," *Issues in Science and Technology*, Winter 1995–96, p. 52.

Chapter Three

1. Charles Heckscher, *White-Collar Blues: Management Loyalties in an Age of Restructuring* (New York: Basic Books, 1995), p. 183. Reprinted with permission of Basic Books, a member of Perseus Books, L.L.C.

2. "Toward a Methodology to Measure the Contribution of Space," report prepared by DFI International, Washington, D.C., December 19, 1998, p. 36.

3. Amy Cortese, "A Census in Cyberspace," *Business Week*, May 5, 1997, p. 84.

4. Charles McGrath, "The Internet's Arrested Development," *New York Times Magazine*, December 8, 1996, p. 80.

5. Marilyn J. Cohodas, "Government and the Web Frontier," *Governing*, January 1998, p. 42.

6. H. Brinton Milward and Louise Ogilvie Snyder, "Electronic Government: Linking Citizens to Public Organizations Through Technology," *Journal of Public Administration Research and Technology*, April 1996, p. 267.

7. "The Core and the Cloud," *Economist*, October 4, 1997, Survey Universities, p. 20.

8. James Traub, "Drive-Thru U: Higher Education for People Who Mean Business," *New Yorker*, October 20 and 27, 1997, pp. 114–116.

9. Diana G. Oblinger and Sean C. Rush, eds., *The Learning Revolution: The Challenge of Information Technology in the Academy* (Bolton, Mass.: Anker, 1997), p. 240.

10. Oblinger and Rush, *The Learning Revolution*, p. 8.

11. Louisa Wah, "An Executive's No. 1 Fear," *Management Review*, January 1998, p. 8.

12. T. S. Peric, "Surviving Job Change," *IndustryWeek*, February 19, 1996, p. 57.

13. Peric, "Surviving Job Change," p. 57.

14. Michael Mandel and Toddi Gutner, "Your Next Job," *Business Week*, October 13, 1997, p. 65.

15. Louisa Wah, "The New Workplace Paradox," *Management Review*, January 1998, p. 7.

16. This interview, which took place in 1996, was part of the same benchmarking project that produced the interview with the printer in Chapter Two.

17. Ray Sata, "Organizational Learning—The Key to Management Innovation," *Sloan Management Review*, Spring 1989, p. 64.
18. Jeanne C. Meister, *Corporate Quality Universities: Lessons in Building a World-Class Work Force* (Burr Ridge, Ill.: Irwin/ ASTD, 1973), p. 13.
19. Heckscher, *White-Collar Blues*, p. 183.

Chapter Four

1. Office of Technology Assessment, *Electronic Enterprises: Looking Toward the Future* (Washington, D.C.: U.S. Government Printing Office, 1994), p. 10.
2. The development of the flexible organization is detailed in John G. Sifonis and Beverly Goldberg, *Corporation on a Tightrope: Leadership, Governance, and Technology in an Age of Complexity* (New York: Oxford University Press, 1996).
3. Stephen Baker and Amy Barrett, "Calling All Nerds," *Business Week*, March 10, 1997, p. 36.
4. "The Rebirth of IBM," *Economist*, June 6, 1998, pp. 65–68.
5. Stephen A. Herzenberg, John A. Alic, and Howard Wial, *New Rules for a New Economy: Employment and Opportunity in Postindustrial America, A Twentieth Century Fund Book* (Ithaca, N.Y.: ILR Press, 1998). This book presents an in-depth look at the service sector economy and the range of jobs involved in it, including the changes that have taken place within the job categories encompassed by the words *service sector*.
6. "The End of Jobs for Life," *Economist*, February 21, 1998, p. 76.
7. Paul Osterman, *Securing Prosperity: The American Labor Market* (Princeton, N.J.: Princeton University Press, 1999), Chapter Five.
8. Shoshana Zuboff, *The Age of the Smart Machine: The Future of Work and Power* (New York: Basic Books, 1988), p. 31.
9. Amy Harmon, "With Boom in High Technology, Software Jobs Go Begging," *New York Times*, January 13, 1998, p. A1.
10. Gene Koretz, "Be Your Own Boss, Earn Less?" *Business Week*, November 28, 1994, p. 32.

Chapter Five

1. Frank K. Sonnenberg, *Managing with a Conscience: How to Improve Performance Through Integrity, Trust, and Commitment* (New York: McGraw-Hill, 1994), p. 129.

2. U.S. Congress, Office of Technology Assessment, *Electronic Enterprises: Looking to the Future*, OTA-TCT-600 (Washington, D.C.: U.S. Government Printing Office, May 1994), p. 5.

3. Henri-Jean Martin, "The Power of the Pen," *UNESCO Courier*, April 1995, pp. 26–27.

4. Elizabeth L. Eisenstein, *The Printing Press as an Agent of Change: Communications and Cultural Transformations in Early-Modern Europe* (New York: Cambridge University Press, 1979). Originally published in two volumes, this book is now available in a single paperback volume. It offers the reader an education on how to understand the effects of change on the world. Every time you read it, you find yourself deep in thought.

5. John Brooks, *Telephone: The First One Hundred Years* (New York: HarperCollins, 1976), p. 8.

6. Brooks, *Telephone*, p. 115.

7. Claude S. Fischer, *America Calling: A Social History of the Telephone to 1940* (Berkeley: University of California Press, 1992), p. 42.

8. Fischer, *America Calling*, p. 22.

9. Peter Keen, *Every Manager's Guide to Information Technology* (Boston: Harvard Business School Press, 1991), p. 94. A second edition of this invaluable book was published in 1994. Keen has also prepared guides to the Internet and telecommunications. His clear explanations are a wonderful place to start learning the language used by the experts in these fields; once the language makes sense, instructions in manuals are much easier to follow.

10. Paul Glister, *Digital Literacy* (New York: Wiley, 1997), p. 7.

11. Walter Wriston, "The Decline of the Central Bankers," *New York Times*, September 20, 1992, p. F11.

12. Ed Ayers, "The Expanding Shadow Economy," *World Watch*, August 1996, p. 11.

Chapter Six

1. Reprinted with permission of the publisher. From *Rewiring the Corporate Brain: Using the New Science to Rethink How We Structure and Lead Organizations*, p. 123, copyright © 1997 by Danah Zohar, Berrett-Koehler Publishers, Inc., San Francisco, CA. All rights reserved. 1-800-929-2929.
2. Paul Hoffman, "Internet Electronic Mail," *Scientific American*, March 1998, p. 108.
3. W. Brian Arthur, "Wonders," *Scientific American*, February 1997, p. 107.
4. Frank K. Sonnenberg's *Marketing to Win* (New York: Harper-Collins, 1990), Chapter Six, presents a detailed examination of the hows and whys of old-style business networking.
5. John Huey, "The New Post-Heroic Leadership," *Fortune*, February 21, 1994, p. 44.
6. "Firms That Never Sleep," *Economist*, January 10, 1998, p. 16.
7. Jenny Leach, "Teacher Education—Online?" *Education Leadership*, 54(3), November 1996, p. 69.
8. Herb Brody, "Wired Science," *Technology Review*, October 1996, p. 49.
9. John Perry Barlow, "The Best of All Possible Worlds," *Communications of the ACM*, 40(2), February 1997, p. 73.
10. Barlow, "The Best of All Possible Worlds," p. 73.
11. The book mentioned is Chuck Martin, *The Digital Estate: Strategies for Competing, Surviving, and Thriving in an Internetworked World* (New York: McGraw-Hill, 1997), Chapter Sixteen. One of the best articles on this subject is Jenny C. McCune's "E-mail Etiquette," *Management Review*, April 1997, pp. 14–15. Once you are connected to the Internet, you can do a search for information; simply select a search engine and type in *netiquette*. You will be amazed at the number of places you will find listed that address this subject.

12. As of April 16, 1999, this was available at
    http://www.albion.com/netiquette/introduction.html.

Chapter Seven

1. Sissela Bok, "Grappling with Principles," in *An Agenda for the 21st Century*, edited by Rushworth M. Kidder (Cambridge, Mass.: MIT Press, 1989), p. 12. Reprinted with permission.
2. Richard O. Mason, Florence M. Mason, and Mary Culnan, *Ethics of Information Management* (Thousand Oaks, Calif.: Sage, 1995), p. 1.
3. Ken Shelton, "Cultures of Trust and Truth," *Executive Excellence*, July 1994, p. 2.
4. Michael Maccoby, "Building Trust Is an Art," *Research-Technology Management*, 40(5), September/October 1997, pp. 56–57.
5. Keith H. Hammonds, "Online Insecurity," *Business Week*, March 16, 1998, p. 102.
6. Zina Moukheiber, "Plus ça Change . . .," *Forbes*, February 10, 1997, p. 46.
7. Martha H. Peak, "Is Your Electronic Door Locked?" *Management Review*, September 1996, p. 7.
8. Richard O. Mason, "Four Ethical Issues of the Information Age," *Management Information Systems Quarterly*, 10(1), March 1986, p. 1.
9. Heather Green, "A Little Privacy Please," *Business Week*, March 16, 1998, pp. 98–99.
10. Steve Lawrence and C. Lee Giles, "Searching the World Wide Web," *Science*, 280, April 3, 1998, pp. 98–100.
11. Gary Taubes, "Science Journals Go Wired," *Science*, 271, February 9, 1996, pp. 764–766; Gary Taubes, "Electronic Preprints Point the Way to 'Author Empowerment,'" *Science*, 271, February 9, 1996, pp. 767–768.
12. This version of the "Ten Commandments of Computer Ethics" appears on the institute's Web site: *http://www.cpsr.org/program/ethics/cei.html* (as of April 16, 1999).

Chapter Eight

1. Edward A. Filene, *Speaking of Change: A Selection of Speeches and Articles* (Kingsport, Tenn.: Kingsport Press, 1939), p. 32. Filene made these remarks in a speech before the School of Business Administration at the University of Buffalo on December 9, 1936.
2. Don Tapscott, *The Digital Economy: Promise and Peril in the Age of Networked Intelligence* (New York: McGraw-Hill, 1996), p. 47.
3. Beverly Goldberg and John G. Sifonis, *Dynamic Planning: The Art of Managing Beyond Tomorrow* (New York: Oxford University Press, 1994), p. 102.
4. The author made these observations in the course of a Siberg Associates consulting engagement.
5. Much of this section appears in Beverly Goldberg and John G. Sifonis, "Focusing Your E-commerce Vision," *Management Review*, September 1998, pp. 48–51.
6. Andy Reinhardt, "Log On, Link Up, Save Big," *Business Week*, June 22, 1998, p. 132.
7. I. Jeanne Duggan, "The Baron of Books," *Business Week*, June 29, 1998, p. 115.
8. Source Services Corp, with which the author worked during a Siberg Associates engagement, merged with Romac International, Inc. (based in Tampa, Florida) shortly after going public in 1997. Source became a wholly owned subsidiary under the agreement.
9. I located this information from the American Electronics Association by doing an on-line search; it appeared in a number of places: an article by Tom Diederich, "Report cites a record 4.5 million high-tech workers," posted by *Computerworld* magazine (*http://www.computerworld.com/home/online9697.nsf/all/980520report1F8BE*). The date given was May 20, 1998, and it was still on-line as of April 16, 1999. It also appeared on TechWeb, The Technology News Site, in a number of different releases and articles (*http://www.techweb.com/*). The research took less than an hour.

10. Stephen A. Herzenberg, John A. Alic, and Howard Wial, *New Rules for a New Economy: Employment and Opportunity in Postindustrial America,* A Twentieth Century Fund Book (Ithaca, N.Y.: ILR Press, 1998), pp. 62–63.

11. Marcia Stepanek, "Rebirth of the Salesman," *Business Week,* June 22, 1998, p. 146.

12. Patricia McLagan and Christo Nel, *The Age of Participation: New Governance for the Workplace and the World* (San Francisco: Berrett-Koehler, 1995), p. 104.

13. David M. Gordon, *Fat and Mean: The Corporate Squeeze of Working Americas and the Myth of Managerial "Downsizing"* (New York: Free Press, 1996), pp. 39–40.

14. Stephen Baker and Amy Barrett, "Calling All Nerds," *Business Week,* March 10, 1997, p. 36.

15. John G. Sifonis and Beverly Goldberg, *Corporation on a Tightrope: Leadership, Governance, and Technology in an Age of Complexity* (New York: Oxford University Press, 1996), p. 206.

16. Stanford Sherman, "Are Strategic Alliances Working?" *Fortune,* September 21, 1992, p. 77.

17. Baker and Barrett, "Calling All Nerds," p. 36.

18. Ethan Bronner, "Computer Industry Luring Students into Dropping Out," *New York Times,* June 25, 1998, p. A14.

19. Danah Zohar, *Rewiring the Corporate Brain: Using the New Science to Rethink How We Structure and Lead Organizations* (San Francisco: Berrett-Koehler, 1997), p. 3.

20. Amy Harmon, "With Boom in High Technology, Software Jobs Go Begging," *New York Times,* January 13, 1998, p. A1.

Chapter Nine

1. Edward A. Filene, *Successful Living in the Machine Age* (New York: Simon & Schuster, 1932), p. 71.

2. Michael Specter, "Population Implosion Worries a Graying Europe," *New York Times,* July 10, 1998, p. A6.

3. John Steele Gordon, "What Has Watt Wrought?" *Forbes*, July 7, 1997, pp. 146, 161.
4. Philip B. Evans and Thomas S. Wurster, "Strategy and the New Economics of Information," *Harvard Business Review*, September-October, pp. 74–75.
5. Christopher Farrell, "Why the Productivity Tide Will Lift All Boats," *Business Week*, October 9, 1995, p. 137.
6. Diana G. Oblinger and Sean C. Rush, eds., *The Learning Revolution* (Bolton, Mass.: Anker, 1997), pp. 3–4.
7. Doris Graber, "Disparity in Information Resources: The Widening Gap Between the Rich and the Poor," paper presented at the 1996 San Francisco meeting of the American Political Science Association.
8. Peter Cappelli and others, *Change at Work* (New York: Oxford University Press, 1997), p. 182.
9. Louise Nameth, "A Safety Net for Net Surfers," *Business Week*, April 15, 1996, p. 108.
10. "Roundtable: The Future of Computing and Telecommunications," *Issues in Science and Technology*, Spring 1997, pp. 71–72.

Acknowledgments

Once again, the people to whom I owe a debt of gratitude are numerous. To my coauthor of two previous books, business partner, and dearest friend, John G. Sifonis, I am grateful for opening the world of business to me. For a greater understanding of the new technologies and a chance to meet with people who are part of that world, I am indebted to numerous individuals at Oracle. I am also indebted to the many people I met in technology departments at hospitals, universities, and other nonprofits as part of a benchmarking engagement with Brigham & Women's Hospital in Boston; to the people at Source Services of Dallas, whom I met in the midst of a corporate change that had remarkable results; and to the employees of Bowne & Company in New York (especially the chief technology officer at the time I was there, John A. Stone).

So many people helped at different stages of the writing of this book: Richard O. Mason, who has critiqued the manuscript at every stage, providing sound guidance and insight; Tom Brown of Management General, who has been a friend and adviser throughout—he was the first person I interviewed for this book; and Frank K. Sonnenberg of Sonnenberg, Haviland & Partners, a marketing group that is the epitome of a modern, flexible organization, who has been there from the beginning. In addition, I want to thank Sandra Winicur for her genuinely uplifting and supportive advice, and Wendy Mercer for being there whenever needed.

The Century Foundation, formerly the Twentieth Century Fund, has been my intellectual home for more than two dozen years. I owe an enormous debt to Richard C. Leone, president of the foundation, for his support for my writing over the years; he believes that leadership involves ensuring that employees can seize opportunities for personal growth, and he walks that talk. Members of the staff at the foundation have been most helpful and supportive, particularly Jason Renker, Rashida Valvassori, and Sarah Wright.

My grateful appreciation to Sally Heinemann of *Bridge News;* some of the ideas in this book originally appeared as op-ed pieces I did for her (with the help, advice, and editing of John Fulton). Barbara Ettorre of *Management Review* has also been of enormous help; some of the ideas in this book first appeared in her magazine. Ken Shelton of *Executive Excellence* has also published some of the material that appears here in somewhat different forms.

Special thanks are owed to Meg Janifer, who provided a superb edit of the manuscript, especially the sections related to the Internet; Betsy Feist, who helped construct and shape the tips for each chapter; Kirstin Alfano of Sonnenberg, Haviland & Partners, who prepared the original graphics; and Trina King, who indexed the book.

And, of course, I want to thank a number of people at Jossey-Bass: Alan Schrader, who said the original, rather sketchy outline had great merit and introduced me to Larry Alexander, who acquired the project, and Susan Williams, who has shepherded it through the editing process with grace—and strength. In addition, I want to thank the people at Jossey-Bass who took care of the many, often unrecognized, jobs that go into making a book as easy to read as possible: Pamela Berkman, Hilary Powers, and Alisa Raymond.

About the Author

Beverly Goldberg is vice president of The Century Foundation (formerly the Twentieth Century Fund), a not-for-profit New York–based think tank, and executive vice president of Siberg Associates, Inc., a management consultancy.

She has conducted assignments for a variety of clients such as Oracle Corporation, Brigham and Women's Hospital, Princeton University Press, Shell Oil, Aetna, Ernst & Young, Aquila, Bowne & Co., Inc., and A.T. Kearney, Inc.

She is a coauthor of *Dynamic Planning: The Art of Managing Beyond Tomorrow* (Oxford University Press, 1994) and *Corporation on a Tightrope* (Oxford University Press, 1996), and her articles have appeared in the *Journal of Business Strategy, Management Review, IndustryWeek, Executive Excellence, Director's Monthly,* and the *Journal of Training and Development.* Her shorter opinion pieces have appeared in various newspapers throughout the United States and on the Bridge Newswire.

She can be reached at *goldberg@tcf.org.*

Index

A

A. T. Kearny, Inc., 137
Acceptance of technological change, 17,
   19, 26, 27; tips for, 45, 75
Adapting to technological change, xvi,
   2–3, 5, 17, 19–25, 29, 100, 132,
   143–151
Advanced Research Projects Agency
   (ARPA), 87
Age: and employment, 1, 28, 68, 70, 163;
   and learning, 41–42; and technology,
   xiv, 1–2 , 29
Age of the Smart Machine (Zuboff), 62
Agriculture, 61, 62, 63–64, 65, 72, 83, 157
Alice in Wonderland (Carroll), 47
Amazon.com (company), 88, 119, 139
America Online, 88
American Electronics Association,
   141–142
American Management Association, 118
American Society for Training and Devel-
   opment, 161
Ampère, André-Marie, 82
Anatomy of Fire (Brown), 164
Anxiety: about change, xiii; about trust,
   112. See also Technological anxiety
ARPANET, 87
Arthur, W. Brian, 99–100
AT&T Corp., 49–50
Automobile industry, 55, 60, 82, 138, 157
Ayres, Ed, 89–90

B

Babbage, Charles, 84
Barlow, John Perry, 105
Barnes & Noble Books, 139–140

Barnesandnoble.com (company), 139, 140
Behavior, 17, 99–100, 112–113; in elec-
   tronic communications, 96, 106–108;
   organizational, 116–117, 121, 145
Being Digital (Negroponte), xv
Bellcore (Bell Communications Research,
   Inc.), 163
Benetton SpA, 137
Bessemer, Henry, 82
Beug, James L., 149
Bok, Sissela, 111
Boundary management, 104, 148
Brainstorming, 21, 146
Brody, Herb, 104
Brooks, John, 77–80
Brown, Tom, 163–164, 165
BRP. *See* Business process reengineering
Bueil, Honorat de, 11
Business, 2; attitudes toward, 1, 35; changes
   in, 5–6, 36–37, 48, 53–56, 72, 131–139,
   153; and technology, 48–49, 53, 57–59,
   79, 88, 134–137, 139–141, 143
Business ethics, 116–117, 118–119
Business etiquette, 96; on the Internet,
   106–108
Business information, 35–36
Business process reengineering (BRP),
   132–136, 137
Business strategy, 40, 49–51, 103, 139–140

C

Cable television, 79
Camden (N.J.), 31
Campbell, Van, 148
Career changes, 43; effect of technology
   on, 12–15, 37–38, 39–40, 66, 76–77,
   144–145

CareerNet, 37
Carroll, Lewis, 47
Century Foundation, The, 165–166
Change, xiii, 153. *See also* Business,
  changes in; Organizational structure,
  changing; Technological change;
  Technology, and change
Chat groups (Internet), 113–114
Citibank, 89
Clinton administration, 150
Colleges and universities, 149; role of,
  33–34; use of technology by, 31–34,
  164–165
Commerce Department (U.S.), 150
Communication, 55, 101, 108, 138. *See
  also* Networking
Communications technology, 86, 87,
  155–156; in business, 24, 132–133;
  social aspects, xiii-xiv, 2, 8, 29, 79,
  80–81. *See also* Electronic commun-
  ication
Competition, 48–51, 54–55, 132, 153
Computer Ethics Institute, 126
Computer industry, 24–25, 59, 83–85,
  157, 162, 163
Computer networks, 155–156. *See also*
  Internet
Computer revolution, 1–2, 83–85
Computers, 155; attitude towards, 24–25;
  in business, 58–59, 74, 85, 88, 134;
  ethical use of, 126–127; history of,
  84–85; personal use of, 6, 7, 29, 30, 56,
  83, 90. *See also* Internet
Connectivity. *See* Electronic connectivity;
  Interpersonal relations; Networking
Contingent workers, 19–20, 23, 49, 147
Continuous learning, 34, 35, 40–42, 161
Coping: with reinventing skills, 151; with
  trust, 129. *See also* Adapting to tech-
  nological change
Core competencies of business, 49, 160
Core workers, 19, 20, 53, 60, 67, 147
Corporate culture, 9, 103, 116–117
Corporate loyalty, 4, 47, 49, 103
Corporate networking, 96; problems in,
  102–104
Creativity, 64–65, 69, 72, 75, 146, 160
Credit card fraud, 117, 118
Cross training, 41, 159
Cultural differences, 112–113
Customer relations, 50, 51, 54, 56, 57,
  136–137, 144, 145, 160
Cyberspace, xv, 105. *See also* Internet

D

Defense Department (U.S.), 66, 87
Deming, W. Edwards, 138
DFI Incorporated, 28–29
Digital Economy, The (Tapscott), 132
Displaced workers, 1, 3, 12–14, 37, 41, 83,
  147. *See also* Job loss
Distance learning, 32, 33–34
Domain names, 88–89
Dow Corning Corp., 148
Downsizing, 41, 50, 133–134; anxiety
  about, xiv, 1, 47, 49
Drake, Edwin Laurentine, 82
Drucker, Peter, 32
DST Systems Inc., 135

E

E-commerce. *See* Electronic commerce
E-mail, 29, 88, 121–122
Earnings, 3, 43, 49, 63, 66, 160, 162; in
  technology jobs, 40, 142
EDI. *See* Electronic data interchange
Edison, Thomas A., 82
Education, 32–33, 76–77, 149, 161–162;
  using technology in, 25–26, 31–34,
  150, 162, 164–165
Efficiency, industrial, 31, 55, 56, 79
Eisenstein, Elizabeth L., 76, 171 n4
Electricity: history of, 81, 82–83, 84, 85
Electronic books, 164–165
Electronic commerce, 90, 137, 138–141,
  147, 160; security issues, 117–118, 119
Electronic communication, 30, 53, 57,
  89–90, 104, 143–145. *See also* Internet
Electronic connectivity, xiii-xiv, xvii, 8,
  111, 163, adaption of, 28–30, 109,
  164; ethical issues, 23, 112, 116–117,
  118, 126, 128, 157–158; social aspects,
  xv. *See also* Electronic networking
Electronic data interchange (EDI), 133,
  136–137
Electronic Frontier Foundation, 105
Electronic leveraging, 165
Electronic networking, 13–14, 15, 22, 36,
  96, 98–99, 101–102; in business,
  102–104, 109, 114–116, 159; problems
  in, 102–103, 113; rules for, 104–108
Electronic town hall, 31
Ellison, Larry, 148
Elsevier Science Publishers, 125
Emoticons (in e-mail), 106–107
Employability, 3, 33, 40, 47–48, 161

Employees. *See* Workers
Employment, 24, 56, 60,143; effect of
    technology on, 47, 49, 57, 59, 142,
    145, 157; types of, 19–20, 23, 49, 52,
    66, 67–68, 69, 147. *See also* Age, and
    employment; Job creation; Unemploy-
    ment; Workforce
Energy companies, 50
ENIAC (Electrical Numerical Integrator
    And Calculator), 84
Entertainment: use of technology in, 80,
    86, 90, 114
Entrepreneurs, 51–53, 65, 66, 68, 132, 142
Etiquette, 96, 106–107, 109
Eudora (software package), 88
Evans, Philip B., 160
*Every Manager's Guide to Information Tech-
    nology* (Keen), 171 *n9*
Executives, 40, 105–106, 134, 148; job
    loss by, 35, 58; responsibilities of,
    116–117, 145–147. *See also* Middle
    management

F

Face-to-face meetings, 8, 101, 104, 115
Faraday, Michael, 82
Federal Aviation Agency (U.S.), 31
Federal Express Corp., 144
Federal Trade Commission (U.S.), 120
Filene, Edward A., xiii, 16, 131, 132, 153,
    165,166, 167 *n1*
Finance departments, 41, 58–59, 84
Financial planning, 43, 45
Financial sector, 78, 89; security issues in,
    117, 119
Fischer, Claude, 79
Fitzgerald, Gail, 66
Flattened organizations, 142
Flexible organizations, 9, 19, 20, 50–53, 59–
    61, 70, 111, 159–160; problems with,
    102–104; responsibility in, 42–43, 147
Flexible production, 48, 51–53, 62
Forecasting change, 8, 73–74, 79, 89–91,
    93, 153–154
Forrester Research, 117, 139
Fortune 1000 corporations, 118, 120
Framework for overcoming technological
    anxiety. *See* Steps to overcoming tech-
    nological anxiety
Freedom of information, 86–87, 89–90, 158
Friends Provident, 134–136
Furler, Christine, 37

G

Gates, Bill, 148
General Electric Co., 68
Gerstner, Lou, 56
Gibbs, William, 32–33
Global economy, 47, 48, 49, 50, 89–90, 153
Goods sector, 56–57. *See also* Manufactur-
    ing
Gordon & Glickson, 120
Gore, Al, 86
Government : technology development
    by, 87, 126, 150; technology use by, 25,
    31, 57–58, 90
Graber, Doris, 161–162
Graphic user interface (computer), 85
Great Britain, 157
Gutenberg, Johannes, 76

H

Habits, 17. *See also* Behavior
Hammer, Michael, 133
Hanson, Ward, 145
Heckscher, Charles, 27, 43
Henry, Joseph, 82
Home computers. *See* Personal computers
Home Depot, 160
Home pages, 29
Home Shopping Network, 28
Hospital work, 12–15
Huey, John, 102
Hugo, Victor, 1, 9
Human nature, 99–100, 112–113, 156,
    163. *See also* Behavior
Human resources, 103. *See also*
    Workforce

I

IBM, 24–25, 33, 49, 56, 84
Income distribution, 162
Independence in work, 66, 68, 69
Industrial age, xiii, 61, 62, 63, 64, 65, 72,
    157
Industrial revolution, 81–83, 153
Information, 48; accuracy of, 21, 120, 122,
    123–125, 129; collection of, 35–36,
    71, 75–77, 118, 155–156; communica-
    tion of, 53, 55, 77–79, 80–81, 86, 88,
    155–156; searching for, 98–99, 115,
    122–123; sources for, 80, 86, 98, 158;
    spread of, 76–77. *See also* Electronic
    connectivity

Information age, 3, 61, 62–63, 64–65, 66, 83–92
Information Anxiety (Wurman), 21
Information superhighway, 86
Information technology, 14, 155; in business, 24, 58–59, 66, 132–133, 134–135, 137, 145, 147; social aspects, xiii-xiv, 2
Information Technology Association, 147
Insurance companies, 3, 50, 58–59, 134–136, 144, 145
Internal Revenue Service (U.S.), 31
International Monetary Fund, 3
Internet, 7, 29, 98, 102, 112–115, 122–125; attitudes toward, 117, 118; business use of, 104, 120, 137, 142–143, 148–149; educational use of, 164–165; explaining, 86–92; rules for use, 104–108, 109, 172 n11. *See also* E-mail; World Wide Web
Internet revolution, 161–162
Internet service providers, 88–89
Interorganizational relations, 111, 116–117, 148; effect of technology on, 53, 90, 104,112, 118–119, 136–138. *See also* Customer relations; Supplier relations
Interpersonal relations, 8, 45, 55, 95, 103, 111, 159. *See also* Electronic connectivity; Face-to-face meetings; Networking; Team work

J

Job assessment, 37, 38–39, 45, 151
Job creation, 2, 6, 20, 40, 137, 141–142, 145, 147–149. *See also* Employment
Job listings, 38–39, 141
Job loss, 1, 3, 5–6, 35, 56, 58, 59, 66, 83, 145. *See also* Displaced workers; Downsizing; Layoffs; Unemployment
Job recruiters, 36, 39, 140–141
Job satisfaction, 38, 66
Job security, xiv, 1, 36, 47, 56, 59–60, 65, 66

K

Kapor, Mitch, 105
Karat, Clare-Marie, 24–25
Katzenbach, Jon R., 138
Keen, Peter, 171 n9

Knowledge: accumulating, 17, 20–22, 35–36, 71, 86, 115–116, 144–145 ; tips for, 93. *See also* Information
Knowledge work, 131–132, 150, 160

L

Labor Department (U.S.), 150
Lao-tzu, 20–21
Larsen, Flemming, 3
Layoffs, 60, 68, 134. *See also* Downsizing
Leadership, 116–117, 147, 151, 164. *See also* Management
Lean companies, 147, 160
Leibniz, Gottfried Wilhelm von, 83–84
Lenoir, Etienne, 82
Lifetime employment. *See* Job security

M

Machiavelli, Niccolo, 16
Machine age. *See* Industrial age
Mainframe computers, 84, 134
Management, 36, 50, 53–54, 63–64, 65, 145–146, 148; and technology, 103, 135–136, 143, 146–147
Manufacturing, 51–53, 54–56, 62, 81–83, 131, 136–137, 138
Manufacturing companies, 50, 57
Martin, Henri-Jean, 72
Mason, Richard O., 120
Mass media: hyperbole, xv-xvi, 7, 21; and technology, 98–99
McGrath, Charles, 29
McKinsey & Company, 138
Medical information, 119, 158
Mental energy, 17, 63
Mergers and acquisitions, 35
"MG" Web site, 164, 165
Microsoft Corporation, 148
Middle managers, 55, 146, 159; displacement of, 1, 41, 74, 131, 136, 145–146
Military: technology use by, 28–29, 54, 66, 84, 87
Millennium, xvii
MILNET, 87
Mining, 81–82
MIT Laboratory for Computer Science, 163
Modem (computer), 87, 88
Motorola, Inc., 138, 150
Murphy, Kevin, 161

N

National Planning Association, 162
Negroponte, Nicholas, xv, 7
Net. *See* Internet
"Net boxes," 88
Netiquette, 106, 172 n11
Netiquette (Shea), 107
Netscape, 88
Networking, 17, 21–22, 36, 39, 95–96,
    97–98, 115, 142; flexibility in, 101; in
    organizations, 96, 102–104; principles
    of, 100–101; tips for, 109. *See also* Elec-
    tronic networking
New York City (N.Y.), 31

O

Oblinger, Diana G., 33
Oersted, Hans Christian, 82
Operating systems (computer), 85
Oracle Systems Corp., 148
Organizational boundaries, 104, 111, 148.
    See also Interorganizational relations
Organizational learning, 132
Organizational structure, 40, 50, 54–55,
    62–63, 69, 143; changing, 2, 11, 47,
    53–58, 72, 131, 159–160, 162; size, 2,
    20, 67; virtual, 51–53. *See also* Busi-
    ness; Corporate culture; Flexible orga-
    nizations; Workplace
Outsourcing, 20, 23, 49–50, 60, 111,
    114–116, 160

P

Paperwork: reducing, 134–136, 137
Parsons, Charles, 82
Pascal, Blaise, 83
Part-time workers, 19–20, 28, 53, 57, 68
Pepper, Jerry, 164–165
Permanent workers. *See* Core workers
Perot, H. Ross, 31
Personal computers, 7, 83, 90, 122
Personal networks, 95, 96–97, 100–101,
    102, 103. *See also* Networking
Pharmaceutical companies, 137
Physical energy, 63
Poor, 157; access to technology, 11,
    25–26, 161–163
Printing: effect of technology on, 12–14,
    18, 76–77
Privacy: protecting, 105, 116, 117,
    119–120, 121–122, 129, 158

Privacy and American Business (newslet-
    ter), 120
Production. *See* Manufacturing
ProfNet (service), 98
Progress, 1, 9

Q

Quality teams, 138

R

Radio, 87; spread of, 30, 79, 80
Reengineering. *See* Business process
    reengineering
"Reengineering Work: Don't Automate,
    Obliterate" (Hammer), 133
Reinvention: business, 133–143; of skills,
    11, 14, 17, 23–25, 131–132; tips for,
    151
Relationships, 8, 111. *See also* Interorgani-
    zational relations; Interpersonal rela-
    tions; Networking
Reputation, 23, 16, 119
Responsibility, 156; managerial, 116–117,
    145–147; organizational, 42–43, 103,
    120; of workers, 20, 40–42, 48, 64, 147
Résumés, 38
Retirement, 28, 163
Rewards of work, 65–66, 148, 160. *See also*
    Earnings
Riggio, Leonard, 139–140
Robert Half International, 35
Rothschild, Nathan, 77, 78
Rush, Sean C., 33
Rust, Mary Anne, 37

S

Sata, Ray, 42
Science fiction, 73–74
Search engines (Internet), 122, 123
Sears, Roebuck and Co., 49
Security issues, 23, 105–106, 116,
    117–121, 129, 158
Self-employment, 66, 68. *See also* Entre-
    preneurs
Service sector, 51, 56, 57, 62, 83,
    131–132, 170 n5
Shea, Virginia, 107
Silicon Alley (N.Y.), 142
Silicon Valley (Calif.), 42, 142 148, 162
Six degrees of separation, 96–97. *See also*
    Networking

Skills: changing, xiv, 5–6, 37–38, 60,
131–132, 138; competence in, 19, 20,
143, 144, 146, 147; importance of, 47,
132, 143, 148; learning, 1, 11, 14–15,
17, 40–42, 47–48, 67, 143–145, 150,
161; limits of, xiv-xv, 20–21, 75–76
Small Business Administration (U.S.), 20
Smith, Douglas K., 138
Sonnenberg, Frank K., 71
Speculation about change. *See* Forecasting change
Stakeholders, 22, 104–105
Steps to overcoming technological anxiety, xviii, 11, 17–18, 19–26, 27, 47–48,
71, 95–96, 111, 131–132
Success Training Institute, 37
Supplier relations, 136–137, 147–148, 160

T

Tapscott, Don, 132
Team work, 55, 64, 71, 96, 133, 138,
147–148, 159; electronic, 22, 23;
problems with, 104, 138, 143
Technological anxiety, 1–2, 29, 34,
149–150; overcoming, xviii-xix, 17,
26, 27, 47–48, 71, 95–96, 111,
131–132; privacy issues in, 119–120,
121; tips for overcoming, 45, 69, 93,
109, 129, 151
Technological change, xvii, 78, 93,
131–132, 153, 163; and education,
31–34, 161–162, 164–156; myths and
reality about, xv-xviii, 4–8; social
aspects, 6, 8, 72–73, 74–75, 78–79,
80–83, 90, 156–157, 161–163. *See also*
Acceptance of technological change;
Adapting to technological change;
Understanding technological change
Technological skills, 1, 2, 39–40, 59,
131–132, 148–149, 161
Technology: and change, xvii, 6–7, 90,
153; learning, xx, 2, 4–5, 39–40, 59,
72–73, 161; spread of, 1, 7, 30–31,
72–73, 77–79, 80. *See also* technology
under subjects, e.g. Business, and technology; Education, using technology
in
Technology careers, 3, 39–40, 142–143,
147, 148–149, 157; training for, 66,
144, 150

Technology companies, 24–25, 56,
141–142
Telecommunications Acts, 11
Telecommuting. *See* Work at home
Teleconferencing: in business, 53; in edu-
cation, 32
Telephone, 86, 87; spread of, 30, 77–79
Temporary workers, 19–20, 23, 52,
67–68
Ten Commandments of Computer Ethics,
The, 126–127
Tesla, Nikola, 82
Thornton, Mac, 164
3M Company, 138
Time, 74, 90; and work, 62–63. *See also*
Flexible organization
Total Quality Management (TQM),
138
Towers Perrin Workplace Index, 40
Toys "R" Us, 160
Trucking industry, 144
Trust: establishing, 17, 36, 112–113; in
electronic relationships, 23, 111,
112–116, 127–128, 157–158; in infor-
mation, 122–125, 158; organizational,
105–106, 116–122; in people, 105,
113–116; in society, 125–126; tips
for establishing, 129
Turing, Alan, 84
Twentieth Century Fund, 165–166

U

Uncertainty about change, xiii, xiv, 160,
161. *See also* Technological anxiety
Understanding technological change,
4–5, 17, 19–20, 22, 47–48, 85; tips for,
69
Unemployment, 2, 147; effect of technol-
ogy on, 1, 3, 13, 15, 147. *See also*
Downsizing; Employment; Job loss;
Layoffs
United States, 80, 125–126; demographic
changes, 25; economy, 3, 20, 25, 57,
78, 131, 150, 157, 161–162
Universities. *See* Colleges and universi-
ties; Virtual universities
University of Minnesota–Duluth,
164–165
University of Phoenix, 32–33
Urbanization, 83

V

Videophones, 79
Virtual companies, 51–53, 68
Virtual universities, 32, 33–34
Volpe, Welty & Co., 139
Volta, Alessandro, 82
Volunteer work, 28
Von Neumann, John, 84

W

Wade, Nicholas, 7
Wages. *See* Earnings
Wall Street, 78, 134
War, 28–29, 77, 80, 84
Watt, James, 81
Web sites, 31, 88, 106, 119, 139, 140–141,
    158, 164, 165
Westin, Alan, 120
White-Collar Blues (Heckscher), 43
*Wisdom of Teams: Creating the High-
    Performance Organization* (Katzenbach
    and Smith), 138

Women: and work, 58–59, 79
Work, 1, 2, 11, 19, 48, 61–66, 90, 160
Work at home, 6, 8, 20, 103
Workers: training, 20, 40, 41–43, 45, 59,
    136, 144; retraining, 11, 49, 66, 150,
    161. *See also* Contingent workers;
    Core workers; Displaced workers;
    Temporary workers
Workplace, 20; changes in, 47–48, 55,
    61–66, 69, 138, 159–161; effect of
    technology on, 5–7, 8, 49, 58–59, 121,
    134–137
Workforce, xiv, 28, 137, 141. *See also*
    Employment; Unemployment
World Wide Web, 89, 122. *See also* Web
    sites
Wriston, Walter, 89
Wurman, Richard Saul, 21
Wurster, Thomas S., 160

Z

Zohar, Danah, 95
Zuboff, Shoshana, 62